# 3-D CITY GUIDES

# MUNICH

# 3-D CITY GUIDES

# MUNICH

## THE COMPREHENSIVE STREET-BY-STREET GUIDE
## WITH BIRD'S-EYE-VIEW MAPPING

Written by Christopher Middleton
Maps created by Irwin Technical Ltd

**DUNCAN • PETERSEN**

Conceived, edited and designed by
Duncan Petersen Publishing Ltd,
54, Milson Road,
London W14 0LB

Sales representation in the United Kingdom and Ireland
by World Leisure Marketing Limited,
117 The Hollow, Littleover, Derby DE3 7BS, U.K.

Distributed by Grantham Book Services,
Alma Park Industrial Estate, Grantham,
Lincolnshire NG31 9SD, U.K.

Printed by Mateu Cromo, Madrid, Spain

Every reasonable care has been taken to ensure the information in
this guide is accurate, but the publishers and copyright holders can
accept no responsibility for the consequences of errors in the text or
on the maps, especially those arising from closures, or those
topographical changes ocurring after completion of the aerial survey
on which the maps are based.

ISBN 1 872576 16 8

# ACKNOWLEDGEMENTS

The author would like to thank the many people who have helped him with his research. Dozens of people gave information about buildings they live or work in: Herr Winkler, Frau Stark and Frau Manhard at the Munich Tourist Information Office, 1 Sendlinger Strasse, gave invaluable help; and of the many publications consulted in the course of writing, the author particularly acknowledges *Knaurs Kulturführer in Farbe: München* (Droemer Knaur).

**Editorial**

| | |
|---|---|
| Editorial director | Andrew Duncan |
| Assistant editor | Joshua Dubin |

**Design**

| | |
|---|---|
| Art director | Mel Petersen |
| Designers | Chris Foley and Beverley Stewart |

Aerial survey by Aeropan, Munich
Maps created by Irwin Technical Ltd,
c/o Irwin Technical (Portsmouth) Ltd, Prudential Buildings,
16 Guildhall Walk, Portsmouth, Hants PO1 2DE

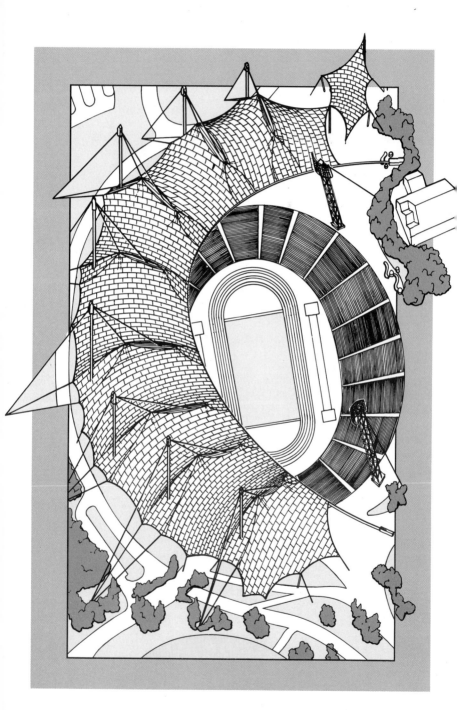

# Contents

The indexes are essential features of these guides. In particular, **the index of points of interest** provides, under convenient and obvious headings such as shops, museums, cafés, bars and restaurants, a quick-reference listing of essential practical and sightseeing information: instant access to the guide and to the city.

# About this book

## How the mapping was made

Isometric mapping is produced from aerial photographic surveys. For this book, aerial photography was provided by Munich specialist, Aeropan.

Scores of enlargements were made from the negatives which Irwin Technical, a group of technical illustrators (address on page 5), then used to create the maps. It took well over 1,000 hours to complete the task.

'Isometric' projection means that verticals are the same height, whether in the foreground or the background - at the 'front' (bottom) of the page or at the 'back' (top). Thus the diminishing effect of perspective is avoided and all the buildings, whether near or distant, are shown in similar detail and appear at an appropriate height.

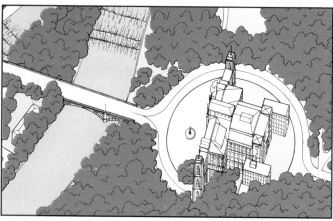

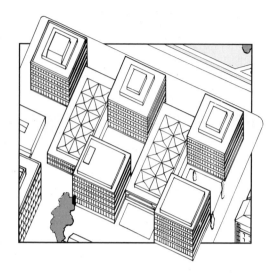

## The order of the maps

The map squares are arranged in sequence running from north to south and from west to east. For further details, see the master location map on pages 32-33.

## Numerals on maps

Each numeral on a map cross-refers to the text printed down the right hand border of the map. The numbers generally read from the top left of each map to the bottom right, in a west-east direction. However, there are deviations from this pattern when several interesting features occur close together, or within one street.

## Opening and closing times

If a museum, display or exhibition is open during regular working hours, opening and closing times are not mentioned in the text accompanying the maps. Brief details are however given when opening times are irregular. In the case of historic or otherwise interesting buildings, assume that you cannot gain access to the interior unless opening times are mentioned.

## Prices
**D**    means one person can eat for less than 30 DM.
**DD**   means one person can eat for less than 60 DM.
**DDD**  one person generally pays more than 60 DM.

Wine or beer is not included. As a rule of thumb, a bottle of wine costs about five times more than a litre of beer.

## Coverage
No guide can hope to cram in everything a city has to offer. This one gives you a particularly rich cross-section of Munich: a mixture of beer and medieval history, of sausage and opera, of smoky wine cellars and wide open parkland. The author has concentrated on aspects of the city brought out by the special nature of the mapping, with emphasis on historical information that helps to explain the fabric, the evolution and the working of the city. He has also tended to draw attention to the outstanding, even to the peculiar, sometimes at the expense of the obvious and well-established, in the belief that this best reveals the character of a city. There is, in addition, much about eating, drinking, shopping and other practical matters.

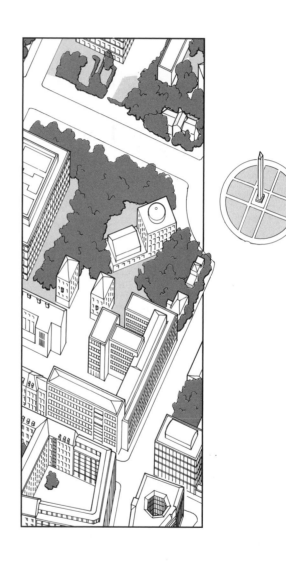

# VISITOR INFORMATION

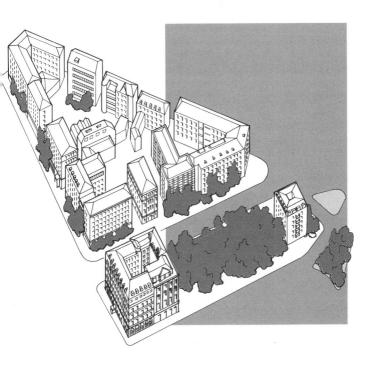

# Munich in a nutshell: the sights you should not miss

These two pages give you instant access to the city. Listed are the 'musts' for every visitor to Munich, plus the map pages where you will find the sights marked, together with descriptions linked to the maps by numerals in circles. No such list can pretend to be complete, or to give a fair picture of a city, but if you have limited time, it will help to use this guide to best advantage.

However, this book can give you something more than easy access to all the major attractions. The way to get to know a city is, of course, to wander the streets, with no great purpose except to enjoy what comes up. This book is ideal for this, for highlighted on the maps are all the features, well-known and little-known, which make Munich special.

Even if you don't feel like walking, just make your way to one of the map squares, find somewhere comfortable to sit, and 'read' the maps, with their accompanying text: this is as near as you can get to drifting over Munich in a ballon, with your own private guide to describe the points of interest.

## Don't miss:

**Alte Pinakothek and Neue Pinakothek, ④, pages 48-9, ①, pages 50-1**. Two of the best art collections in the world.

**Beer cellars**: you must visit at least one of these, for which Munich is justly famous: atmosphere, music, Münchners at their most jolly - and beer out of monstrous glasses. Try the Hofbräuhaus (⑰, **pages 76-7**) or the Mathäser-Bierstadt (⑤, **pages 72-3**).

**The Deutsches Museum, ①, pages 102-03**. A gigantic science museum that is fun as well as instructive.

**The Englischer Garten, pages 54-5**. By any standards one of the largest and most attractive open spaces in a city anywhere. Beer gardens, the rushing River Isar, nude sunbathing.

The magnificent **Frauenkirche, ④, pages 74-5**, with the twin towers, the city's picture-postcard trade mark.

**Königsplatz, ⑤, pages 48-9**. A neo-Classical vision, once the scene of Nazi rallies.

**Views of the Alps**

On clear days, the Alps are visible from the very centre of Munich. These are the best vantage points:
- The Olympic Tower (Olympiaturm) at the Olympiapark (U-bahn Olympiazentrum): an elevator takes you up to a viewing platform 600 feet (180 m) above ground.
- Peterskirche (Rindermarkt): you can climb the stairs to the top of the church tower, 275 feet (80 m).
- Neues Rathaus (Marienplatz): a combination of elevator and stairs takes you to the top of the bell tower, which is 255 feet (80 m) high.
- Frauenkirche (Frauenplatz): there is an elevator to the top of one of the towers - 350 feet (100 m).

**Marienplatz, ⑨, pages 74-5**. The central pedestrian square, and the city's `heart', with the old and new town halls.

**The Michaelskirche, ⑤, pages 74-5,** the **Theatinerkirche, ⑫, pages 64-5, Peterskirche, ⑯, pages 74-5,** and the **Asamkirche, ⑧, pages 84-5**: four very different but outstanding churches, which will fascinate even if you are not especially interested in architecture.

**The Nymphenburg Palace, pages 38-41**, another residence of the Kings of Bavaria, with world-class baroque architecture.

**Odeonsplatz, pages 64-5**. Stroll around this square and drink in the architectural scenery.

**The Oktoberfest, page 95**. The world's biggest beer festival is held in Munich in October. Takes place on the Theresienwiese.

**The Olympic Park, pages 36-7,** with its imposing stadium and soaring tower.

**The Residenz, pages 64-5,** town palace of the former Kings of Bavaria.

**Residenzstrasse, pages 64-5**, and **Maximilianstrasse, pages 76-9**. Browse the expensive shops along these city-centre streets.

**Schwabing, pages 108-09**. Munich's `Left Bank' district, the place to visit for music and nightlife.

**Viktualienmarkt, ⑥, pages 86-7,** Munich's colourful open-air food market.

# Transport

## From airport to city

Munich's former Riem Airport was phased out in May 1992 and replaced by the newly-built Grossflughafen München II (Franz-Josef-Strauss Flughafen), 19 miles (30 km) to the north of the city, near the small town of Erding. The S-Bahn train (line S8) connects the airport with the city's two largest stations, Ostbahnhof (East Station) and Hauptbahnhof (Central Station). Trains leave every 20 minutes and run between 3.20 am and 11.20 pm daily (adults 10 DM, children 2.20 DM). Journey time into the city centre is approximately 40 minutes, which makes the train a much better bet than doing the journey by road.

Special airport buses (adults 12 DM, children 6 DM) leave every 20 minutes for the city centre, between 3.10 am and 9.30 pm every day. The bus deposits you at Arnulfstrasse, on the northern side of the Hauptbahnhof. Here you can transfer to a dozen U-Bahn (underground) and S-Bahn train lines, and as

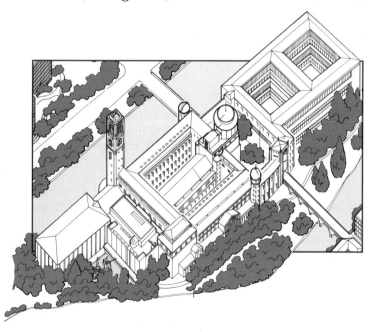

many different tram and bus routes. Journey time on a good day is 45 minutes, but it can stretch to 90 minutes; this area is one of the most traffic-jam prone in Germany, particularly on Friday afternoons.

Taxis from the airport are more expensive (90-100 DM for the journey to the Hauptbahnhof). If you are driving a car yourself, take the A92 from the airport and then join up with the A9. To get to the medieval (and mainly pedestrianized) heart of Munich, look for signs to Altstadtring.

Inside the central airport building, there is a tourist information office (open 8.30 am-10 pm Mon-Sat, and 1 pm-9 pm on Sundays and public holidays; tel. 97592815) and a branch of the Deutsche Verkehrs-Kredit Bank (open 6.30 am-10.30 pm daily). For details of plane departure and arrival times, phone 97521313.

## Trains

Munich has a superbly efficient public transport system, run by the MVV (Münchner Verkehrs-und Tarifverbundes). It runs from around 5 am to 1 am every day. Above ground, there is a reliable bus and tram network; below ground, a clean and swift rail service, consisting of shorter-distance U-Bahn and longer-distance S-Bahn trains. The U-Bahn sign is a white U on a blue background, the S-Bahn a white S on a green background. Tickets are valid for U-Bahn, S-Bahn, tram and bus. The problem is how to buy one.

You have two options. One is to purchase a ticket from a human being. You can do this at any newsagent's or kiosk with a flag or sticker bearing the letter K in green and white.

The other option is to buy a ticket from an automatic machine. These are to be found at all stations. The trick is not to panic when faced with one of these complex-looking creatures. Instead, take a deep breath and ask yourself whether your intended journey counts as a *Kurzstrecke*, or short journey - does your destination appear in the list of places on the far left of the machine, under the heading *Kurzstrecke*? If so, all you need to do is to press the brown button marked 1, which matches the symbol at the top of the *Kurzstrecke* list. Notice that the buttons come in two columns - the left-hand side for adults, the right-hand for dogs and children (four to 14 years old; under four, travel free). When you have pressed the button, the price of your ticket will be automatically displayed.

Now, insert your money. The machines give change, but only accept coins; if you've just got banknotes, don't despair - most of the automatic machines in the centrally located stations now have the capacity to convert 10- or 20-DM notes into coins.

If your destination is not listed as a *Kurzstrecke*, you will need to look at the *Zonen* (circular zone) map, usually displayed alongside the machines. This shows the city divided up into concentric zones. The vast majority of your journeys will take place solely within the central, light blue zone (*Innenraum*), thus counting as a one-zone journey. If this is the case here, press the brown 2 button on the automatic machine. For longer journeys, you can check you are pressing the right button by referring to the longer list of destinations under the heading `ausserhalb von München' (the rest of Munich) and seeing which button is indicated against your stop.

There are a number of money-saving alternatives. A one-day, one-zone card (*Tageskarte*) gives unlimited travel within one zone: if you are going to make more than three one-zone journeys in the day, it is worth buying it. Up to five people (though only two can be over 18) may travel on this one ticket, although not before 9 am on weekdays (this restriction does not apply to solo travellers, who can use it when they want). If you feel confident in your grasp of the system, you can buy a *Mehrfahrtenkarte* (strip ticket), which consists of up to 16 strips; you cancel two strips for every zone travelled, and the card gives you a saving of approximately 25 per cent on the standard single fares.

Once you have got your ticket, make sure you know which line you want and which terminus the train will be travelling towards. For example, if you want to go from Hauptbahnhof to Prinzregentenplatz on the U4 line, you need trains that are travelling in the direction of Arabellapark (Direktion Arabellapark).

At this point, you are almost ready to begin your journey. Your only remaining task is to validate your ticket by inserting it into one of the blue, postbox-like machines marked E. Insert your ticket, wait till it is punched (there may be a bell sound) and then remove it. You will see the time and date has been stamped on it.

By now it may be bedtime, but even if buying your first ticket has been something of an ordeal, don't give up on the train system. The more you use it, the quicker the whole process will become, and it really is the speediest way to get round Munich.

And the fastest way to get into trouble in Munich is to travel on a train without a valid ticket. Prowling the transport system are squads of the MVV's plain-clothes ticket-swoopers, who impose on-the-spot 60-DM fines on travellers found without a valid ticket. These hard-hearted types seem remarkably disinclined to accept ignorance, forgetfulness or even foreign nationality as an excuse.

## Trams and buses

The same zone system applies as with trains. Again you are unlikely to do much straying outside the central blue zone. With trams, you can buy a ticket beforehand from a kiosk displaying the green and white letter K or any automatic machine (most tram and bus stops have them).

Alternatively you can buy a ticket on board; on a bus you have to buy from the driver, on a tram you can buy from either the driver, if the tram is displaying the green and white K symbol, or from the automatic machine which is to be found in the rear carriage of two-carriage trams.

Again, you must remember to cancel your ticket in the blue posting machine: don't rely on some helpful local to remind you.

## Taxis

The taxis in Munich are all a pale yellow colour. You can hail a cab in the street if the light on its roof is illuminated, or else you can pick one up at one of the hundred or more taxi stands in the city.

Alternatively, call the central number (2161-0 or 19410) and for 1 DM extra, a taxi will come and collect you from any point in the city.The hire charge is 3.90 DM; each kilometre (5/8 of a mile) costs 2.20 DM; each piece of luggage and each dog costs 1 DM. Expect to pay at least 10 DM for a short trip in the city.

## Private cars

A car in the middle of Munich is not an asset. Visiting drivers will experience fierce competition for parking spaces, along with rush hour traffic jams on the city's inner and outer ring roads. In addition, large portions of the *Innenstadt* (town centre) are either pedestrianized or else boast one-way systems that perpetually take you further from where you want to go. Many drivers prefer to take advantage of the MVV park-and-ride system, which allows passengers to park their cars free of charge at MVV station car parks. If you do decide to bring your car, you will need to have a valid driving licence, proof of insurance, a national identity sticker for your car, plus a first-aid kit and a red warning triangle in case you break down.

There are several car rental firms in Munich. In the west, Autohansa-Autovermietung is at 10-12 Schiessstattstrasse; tel. 504068. In the north-west, AVM is at 13 Augustenstrasse; tel. 596161; Bayern-Garage at 72 Karlstrasse (near the junction with Seidlstrasse); tel. 591443, and Autoverleih Neuhausen at 300 Arnulfstrasse; tel. 177577. Europcar has different telephone numbers for different parts of town: tel. 557145 (central Munich), tel. 581001 (west), tel. 332525 (Schwabing), tel. 3161033 (north), tel. 435003 (east).

## Bicycles

Specially designated cycle tracks operate through much of Munich, making the bike a much better way to see the city than by car. The biggest bike rental company is Radius Touristik, on the northern side of the Hauptbahnhof, at 3 Arnulfstrasse; tel. 596113. They hire bikes out by the day and by the week.

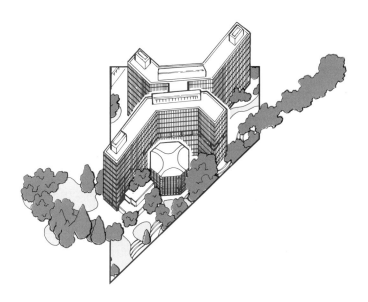

## Beer

There is a strong case for designating beer as a means of transport in Munich. Certainly it helps make the city go round.

Beer halls and beer gardens are an integral part of daily life in Munich. Several thousand drinkers a day weave in and out of the world's biggest beer hall, the Mathäser-Bierstadt, near Karlsplatz, and on a warm day in the Englischer Garten, up to 7,000 people crowd on to the tables around the Chinese Tower. The great breweries such as Löwenbräu and Hofbräu provide jobs for many thousands of Münchners, and so seriously is the subject taken that there is even a faculty of beer at Munich University.

When ordering beer, ask for *Bier vom Fass* (draught), if you want the house brew. *Helles* is the standard, pale-coloured beer, *weissbier* (white beer, made from wheat instead of barley) is the ever-so-slightly-fruity alternative. *Bock* is a strong, malty beer, most widely drunk in the Starkbierzeit, or strong beer season, during the last two weeks in March. *Radlermass* is beer and lemonade, *Russenmass* is *weissbier* and lemonade.

# Visiting Germany

**By train** At Munich's Central Station (Hauptbahnhof) you can pick up direct trains to every major German city and many international destinations, including Italy, Austria and Switzerland. Main-line trains leave from *Gleis* (platforms) 11-26; shorter-distance trains travelling due south towards Wolfratshausen and Tegernsee from platforms 1-10 (also referred to as Holzkirchner Bahnhof); platforms 27-36 (Starnbergerbahnhof) are the departure points for trains travelling towards the Alpine resort of Garmisch-Partenkirchen.

Short-distance trains travelling in an easterly direction leave from the Ostbahnhof (East Station) on the other side of the city.

For general train information, go to the Munich Tourist Information Office (Fremdenverkehrsamt München) in the south of the Hauptbahnhof, adjoining Bayerstrasse, tel. 2391256 and 2391257. It is open Mon-Sat from 8 am to 10 pm, and from 11 am to 7 pm on Sundays. If you want to book a special-rate ticket, a sleeper or a *Tagesrückefahrkarte* (day excursion ticket), go to the *Reisezentrum* inside the Hauptbahnhof. Here you can also buy the full range of German rail cards, which give you unlimited travel on the German rail network for periods of four, nine or 16 days, as well as offering discounts to pensioners and travellers under 26.

**By air** The main airline operator within Germany is Lufthansa. Their main offices in Munich are at 1 Lenbachplatz; tel. 51138. For airport flight information, ring 9772544.

As well as Munich, other international airports in Germany are at Bremen, Cologne, Bonn, Düsseldorf, Frankfurt, Hamburg, Hanover, Nuremberg, Stuttgart and Saarbrücken. All German airports have a bus shuttle service, usually with a terminus at the main rail station.

**By road** Germany has scores of specially designated tourist routes, devised to lead the driver away from the roaring autobahns and through the most picturesque towns, villages and countryside in Germany. The most famous is the *Romantische Strasse* (the Romantic Road), which begins in the attractive baroque town of Würzburg, in Franconia, and bypasses Munich on its 220-mile route to the Alps.

There are four main autobahn routes out of Munich: the A9 north to Nuremberg and south to Garmisch-Partenkirchen (A95) and the A8 west to Stuttgart and east to Salzburg. If you want help with directions, you can consult the *Lotsenstationen* (Driver-Guide Services) at the Ramersdorf exit (to Salzburg) tel. 672755, and the Obermenzing exit (to Stuttgart), tel. 8112412; both are open 8 am-6 pm. News of jams and alternative routes is broadcast on radio channel Bayern 3, frequency 98 MHz. All autobahns are toll free.

If your car breaks down on a minor road, go to the nearest call box, dial 19211 and ask for `road service assistance'. On motorways, two of the three main automobile clubs (ADAC and AvD) operate tow trucks; to call one, use an emergency telephone: there is one every 12 km (7.5 miles). They will pick you up for free, but all labour and parts must be paid for.

You can drive as fast as you like on all German motorways and most people do. In built-up areas, the speed limit is 50 kilometres per hour (30 mph), and on all other roads the limit is 100 kph (60 mph). Seat belts must be worn at all times by both front- and back-seat drivers. Drinking and driving is not advised: the level of alcohol permissible in the blood is 0.8 millilitres (about two glasses of beer), and moves are afoot to reduce the figure to 0.5 ml or lower.

**By bus** Germany's bus network is run by the national railways, and rail tickets (including rail cards and passes) are valid on buses, too. Buses are marked either Bahnbus or Europabus. In Munich, you can buy tickets at the Deutsche Touring GmbH offices in the Hauptbahnhof, next to platforms 27-36, tel. 591824/591825. Trains are mostly quicker at transporting one from A to B, except in the more remote country areas. However, buses do operate along the tourist routes, for example Europabus route 190, which travels from Munich along the Romantic Road to Rothenburg.

**By bike** Germany is a bicycle-friendly country, and Bavaria in particular. Although banned from autobahns, cyclists benefit from bike-only lanes on roads both rural and urban. Bicycles are available for day-hire at large numbers of railway stations, and come at half price if you have a rail ticket. You can return the bike to any other bike-hire station, not just the one you hired it from. If the station does not operate a bike-hiring service, just look in the local phone directory or *Gelbe Seiten* (yellow pages) under *Fahrradverleih* (bicycle hire). You can get information on all aspects of cycling from the *Bund Deutscher Radfahrer* (Association of German Cyclists) at 4 Otto-Fleck-Schneise, 6000 Frankfurt 71.

# Useful data

## Tourist information
Information centres are located at:
- Hauptbahnhof (Bayerstrasse side) open Mon-Fri 8 am-10 pm, Sunday 11 am-7 pm; tel. 2391256.
- Airport (central building) open Mon-Sat 8.30 am-10 pm, Sundays and public holidays 1-9 pm; tel. 97542815.
- Town centre (Rindermarkt/Pettenbeckstrasse) open Mon-Fri 9.30 am-6 pm, closed weekends and holidays; tel. 2391272.
- Karlsplatz underground shopping centre, open Mon-Fri 8 am-6 pm; closed weekends and holidays. tel. 2338242/554459.

For information before you arrive write to:Fremdenverkehrsamt München, Postfach (P.O. Box), 8000 München 1; tel. 23911, fax 2391313.

Recorded telephone information is available 24 hours a day in different languages:

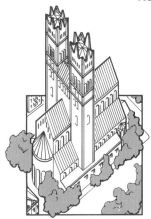

| German | 239161 (museums and galleries) |
| | 239171 (castles and other sights) |
| English | 239162 (museums and galleries) |
| | 239172 (castles and other sights) |
| French | 239163 (museums and galleries) |
| | 239173 (castles and other sights) |

The city's **lost property office** (Fundbüro) is at 19 Ruppertstrasse; tel. 2331. If you lose something on a train (other than an S-Bahn), contact the Fundbüro at the Hauptbahnhof, opposite Platform 26, tel. 1285036. If you leave something on an S-Bahn train, call the relevant office at the Ostbahnhof, tel. 12884409. For property lost in a post office or phone box, ask at the post office at 195 Arnulfstrasse; tel. 12621.

## Sightseeing tours

The main tour operators in Munich are Panorama Tours, next to the Hauptbahnhof, at 8 Arnulfstrasse; tel. 591504. Their blue buses operate throughout the year, leaving from Bahnhofplatz, outside the Hertie department store opposite the Hauptbahnhof. The tours include:

- Mini-tour of the city (*Kleine Rundfahrt*). A one-hour round trip, leaving daily at 10 am and 2.30 pm (plus 11.30 am in mid-summer).

- Olympic Tour (*Olympiagelande-Tour*). Tour of the Olympic Park built to stage the 1972 Olympics. Two-and-a-half hour tour, leaving daily at 10 am and 2.30 pm.
- Full Tour (*Grosse Rundfahrt*) 1. Takes in visits to St Peter's Church and the Alte Pinakothek (*see pages 49, 75*). Two-and-a-half hour tour, leaving Tue-Sun at 10 am.
- Full Tour 2. Takes in visit to the Nymphenburg. Two-and-a-half-hour tour, leaving Tue-Sun at 2.30 pm.
- Munich By Night. Dinner at traditional Bavarian restaurant, visits to night spots and trip up Olympic tower. Wed-Sat, departure at 7.30 pm.
- Royal Castles Tour, including 'mad' King Ludwig II's fairy-tale castle on the clifftops at Neuschwanstein. All-day tour.

More unusual tours are offered by the following companies:
- City Hopper Touren, 95 Hohenzollernstrasse; tel. 2721131. Guided city tours by bicycle. Tue-Sun from 10 am to 6 pm.
- Radius Touristik, Platform 35, Hauptbahnhof; tel. 596113. Guided bicycle tours, Mon, Wed, Fri 10.30 am. Guided foot tours of old city, leave daily 10 am.
- Thematische Stadterkundungen, Postfach (P.O. Box) 401832; tel. 2718940. Tailor-made theme tours for youth and school groups - themes include the River Isar, the Schwabing area (Munich's 'Left Bank'), 'Butchers and Monks'.
- Raft Trips. On summer weekends, large rafts float down the River Isar. Information from the Bavarian Travel Bureau (Amtliches Bayerisches Reisebüro); tel. 59040. Prices from 175 DM per person.
- Tour by taxi. Enterprising taxi driver Raitz von Frentz gives guided tours lasting between one and eight hours. He speaks fluent English and Spanish; tel. 397274.

## Shopping, banking and business hours

Shops in Munich are open from Mon to Fri between 9 am and 6.30 pm and on Saturdays between 8.30 am and 2 pm (6 pm on the first Saturday of the month, known as Langer Samstag). The biggest stores stay open every Thursday until 8.30 or 9 pm. Some bakers and butchers shut up shop on Monday afternoons. All shops are closed on public holidays, except for a few in the shopping centre beneath the Hauptbahnhof, selling bread, cakes, flowers, toiletries and so on. Some of these are also open outside normal shopping hours on working days.

Most banks are open on weekdays from 8 am to 12 pm and 1.30 pm to 3.30 pm (5.30 pm Thursdays). Outside normal banking hours, you can change money 24 hours a day at the Central Post Office in Bahnhofplatz, and at the Deutsche Verkehrs-Kredit-Bank in the Hauptbahnhof, 6 am-11.30 pm.

Most museums are closed on Monday. Normal opening hours, Tues to Sun, are 9 am to 6 pm, with some notable exceptions such as the Bavarian National Museum. Many smaller museums shut for at least an hour at lunchtime. Well worth noting is that entry to all city-run museums is free on Sundays.

Office hours are between 9 am and 6 pm. The rush hour lasts from about 7.30-9 am and 5-7 pm, Mon-Fri.

## Public holidays

Munich has an abundance of public holidays. Shops, offices, banks and restaurants are closed on: New Year's Day (1 January), Epiphany (6 January), Good Friday and Easter Monday (moveable dates), Labour Day (1 May), Ascension Day (9 May), Whit Monday (moveable), Corpus Christi (moveable), Assumption Day (15 August), German Unity Day (3 October), All Saints Day (1 November), Day of Prayer and Repentance (third Wednesday in November), Christmas (25 and 26 December). If a public holiday falls on a Thursday, many shops and offices make a long weekend of it, and take the Friday off, too.

## Festivals

Six million people a year attend the famed/infamous October Beer Festival (Oktoberfest), which runs from the third Saturday in September to the first Sunday in

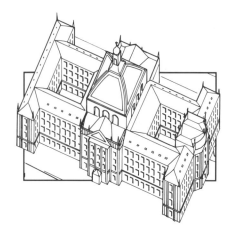

October (nearest U-Bahn stop Theresienwiese). A miniature version, the Spring Festival (Frühlingsfest) takes place on the same showground at the end of April.

The Christmas market (Christkindlmarkt) in the central Marienplatz brings visitors from all over Germany. It begins on the first day of Advent. The new year begins with the colourful carnival season of Fasching, followed by the strong beer season in the second half of March.

## The post

Most post offices (*Postamt*) are open on weekdays between 8 am and 6 pm and on Saturdays between 8 am and 12 pm. The central post office at 1 Bahnhofplatz, tel. 53882732, opposite the main station is open 24 hours a day for posting letters (not parcels), changing money, making long-distance calls and picking up Poste Restante (*Postlagernde*) mail.

## Telephones

You can make international calls from most public phone booths. Look for a sticker saying 'International' or *Auslandsgespräche*. Alternatively, look for a sign showing a black receiver in a green square. Public phones take 10-pfennig, 1-DM and 5-

DM coins. The larger post offices are also good places to make international phone calls if you don't have the right change for phone booths. Go to the counter marked *Fremdgespräche*, where you will be allocated a booth. At the end of your call, return to the counter to pay.

If you are ringing a Munich number from outside the city, the area code is 089. Operator: domestic, tel. 010; international, tel. 0010.

Dialling codes are: to the UK 0044 and to the USA or Canada 001; 0033 to France, and 0031 to the Netherlands.

If you are looking for a particular type of shop or service, refer to the *Gelbe Seiten* (yellow pages) directory. For operator service on a local call, dial 1188; on an international call, 00118. Other useful numbers are:

- Police 110
- Fire 112
- Ambulance 19222
- Babysitter service (multi-lingual) 229291

## Publications

For the most up-to-date and all-embracing listings of forthcoming events and concerts, of theatres, hotels, museums, restaurants and other tourist information buy the inexpensive *Monatsprogramm* (monthly programme). This is published by the Munich Tourist Board and is available (2 DM in 1992) at all tourist information centres, as well as most news-stands and hotels.

The most popular daily newspaper in Munich is the *Münchner Merkur* (Munich Mercury), more down-market than the staid *Süddeutsche Zeitung* (South German News). For a glimpse of alternative Munich, get a copy of the irreverent fortnightly *Münchner Stadtmagazin*.

English-language books can be found most readily at the Anglia English Bookshop, 3 Schellingstrasse, tel. 283642, near the University. In the centre of town, go to the Hugendubel at 22 Marienplatz or 77-79 Amalienstrasse.Newspapers can be bought not only from news-stands and kiosks but also from the unmanned newspaper boxes on most central street corners. Just open the lid and put the correct money in the box.

## Foreign embassies and consulates

Here is a selection of addresses and telephone numbers for foreign embassies, consulates and high commissions. A fuller list is given in the monthly programme (*Monatsprogramm*).

- **Austria** 136 Ismaninger Strasse; tel. 9210900.
- **Belgium** 15 Franz-Joseph-Strasse; tel. 397096/397097.
- **Britain** 62 Amalienstrasse; tel. 3816280.
- **Canada** 29 Tal; tel. 222661.
- **France** 5 Möhlstrasse; tel. 479800.
- **Ireland** 1A Mauerkircherstrasse; tel. 985723.
- **Italy** 3 Möhlstrasse; tel. 4180030.
- **Luxemburg** 99-101 Klenzestrasse; tel. 20242202.
- **Monaco** 14 Von-der-Tann-Strasse; tel. 282718.
- **Netherlands** 1 Nymphenburger Strasse; tel. 594103.
- **Spain** 45 Oberföhringer Strasse; tel. 985027/985028.
- **Switzerland** 33 Leopoldstrasse; tel. 347063/347064.
- **USA** 5 Königinstrasse; tel. 28881

# Medical information

## Emergencies

In the event of an accident or illness, ring the ambulance service (tel. 19222) or the medical emergency service (tel. 558661), who will recommend a doctor to you. In office hours, you can ring the American or British consulates (numbers above) for a list of English-speaking doctors and dentists (*Zahnarzten*).

Citizens of European Community countries are entitled to treatment by the German Health Services, and may be able to have medical expenses (not for prescribed drugs) re-imbursed on their return home. To qualify for this, you must take with you a copy of the correct E111 form from the Department of Health and get German health officials to fill it in as you go along; these forms are available at post offices.

If you are not covered by EC reciprocal arrangements, you should always check whether your present personal insurance arrangements cover you for treatment in Germany. If not, you should take out some short-term holiday medical insurance either with your present insurers or through your travel agent.

## Pharmacies

When closed, pharmacies display a sign giving the address of the nearest one open. You can also find out which are open outside normal hours by ringing the emergency pharmacy number (tel. 594475).

Pharmacies where a range of languages other than German is spoken are as follows:

### Central (Hauptbahnhof) area:
- Bahnhof Apotheke, 2 Bahnhofplatz; tel. 594119/598119.
- Bavaria-Apotheke, 91 Bayerstrasse; tel. 533646.
- City-Apotheke, 9 Schillerstrasse; tel. 555521/555522.
- Europa-Apotheke, 12 Schützenstrasse; tel. 595423.
- Schützen-Apotheke, 5 Schützenstrasse/4 Bayerstrasse; tel. 557661.

### North
- Internationale Lerchen-Apotheke, 201 Schleissheimer Strasse; tel. 3086731.

### South
- Internationale Ludwigs-Apotheke, 8 Neuhauser Strasse; tel. 2603021/2608011.

## Dental treatment

The dental clinic at 70 Goethestrasse (tel. 51600) is recommended by the Munich Tourist Board. For a list of English-speaking dentists, contact the British or American embassies.

# Master location map

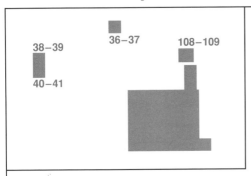

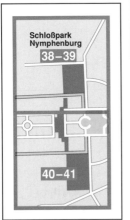

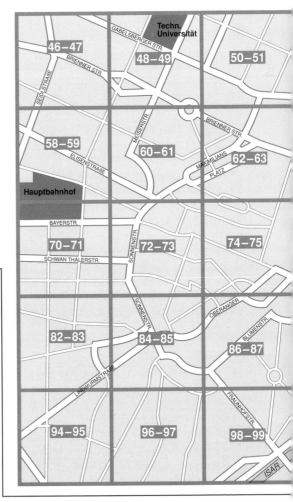

# Master location map

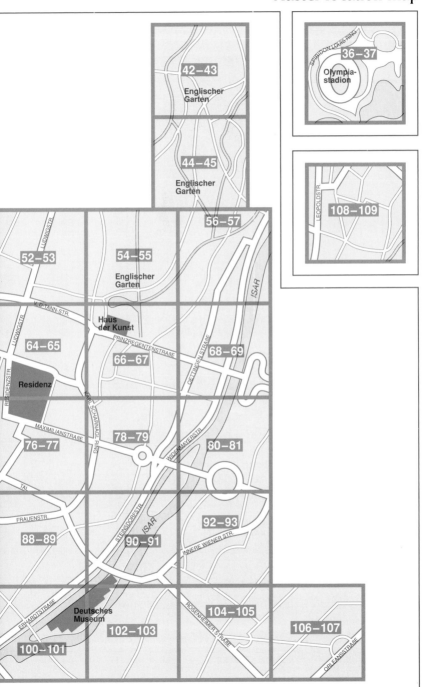

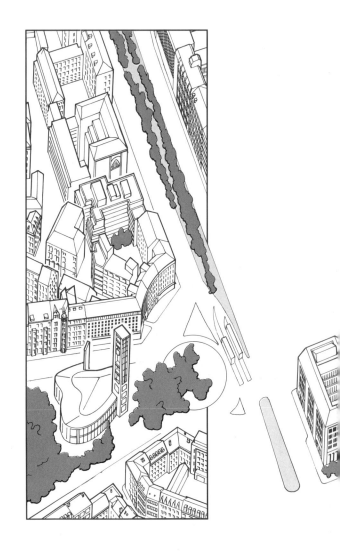

# THE
# ISOMETRIC
# MAPS

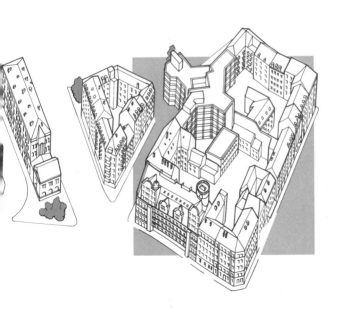

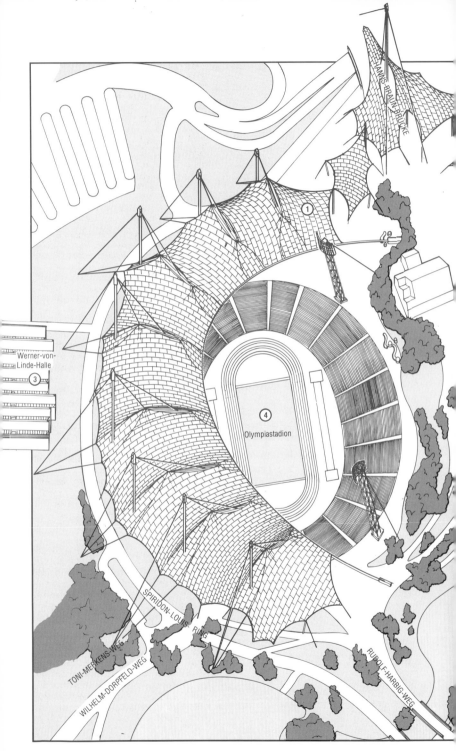

HANNS-BRAUN-BRÜCKE

Werner-von-Linde-Halle

③

①

④

Olympiastadion

SPIRIDON-LOUIS-RING

TONI-MERKENS-WEG

WILHELM-DÖRPFELD-WEG

RUDOLF-HARBIG-WEG

# The Olympic Park

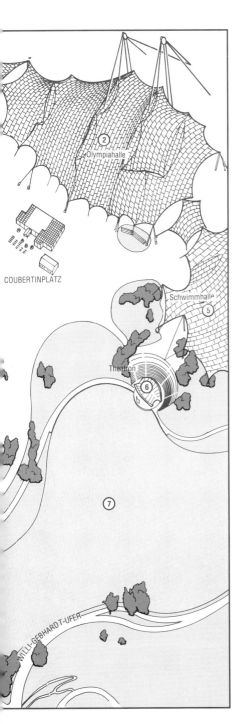

Built on the site of an old military training ground, the Olympic Park rolls for 740 landscaped acres across the northern edge of the city. Built between 1967 and 1972 to stage the 1972 Olympic Games, the complex still has the power to stun with the sheer size and audacity of its architecture. ① The most dramatic feature is the vast, suspended roof - made of tinted acrylic glass. ② During the Games, the 12,000-seater **Olympiahalle** housed most of the big indoor events. Nowadays it is the venue at which all the biggest visiting rock stars play. ③ Werner-von-Linde-Halle contains an entire indoor athletics track: the ceiling is high enough for pole-vaulters to practise. ④ Biggest and best-known of all the sports facilities here is the 80,000-seater **Olympic Stadium**, now the home of top German football team Bayern Munich. The ground's only drawback is that architectural aesthetics have required one side of the stadium to be left uncovered by the roof - with many a wet afternoon the consequence for Bayern fans. ⑤ The **Schwimmhalle** (swimming pool) used in the Olympics is now open to the general public. It has one full-size rectangular pool, a separate diving pool and a sauna. Doors open at 7 am every morning (except Monday) and don't close until 10.30 pm every night. ⑥ The **Theatron** is a small, concrete amphitheatre used for open-air concerts on summer Sundays, beside the artificial **Olympiasee** (Olympic lake) ⑦, on which boats can be hired. You can stroll all round the park on a path which takes you to the site's highest point (200 feet, 60 m), the Olympiaberg, beneath which lie tons of wartime rubble from the city centre. You can get somewhat higher if you go up the 960-foot (300 m) Olympiaturm (Olympic Tower). A lift (5 DM) takes you to a viewing platform 600 feet up, from where (on a clear day) you can see the Alps. There is the Eisstadion (ice stadium), a public ice rink and a Radstadion (velodrome). The Olympic Village, across the ring road to the north, now houses students instead of athletes. During the Games, the women lived in the bungalows (now riotously painted by their new occupants) and the men in the high-rise flats. It was here on 5 September, 1972, that Black September terrorists attacked the Israeli team, killing two team members and taking nine hostage. The episode ended in a disastrous shoot-out: all nine hostages were killed, along with four Arabs and one policeman.

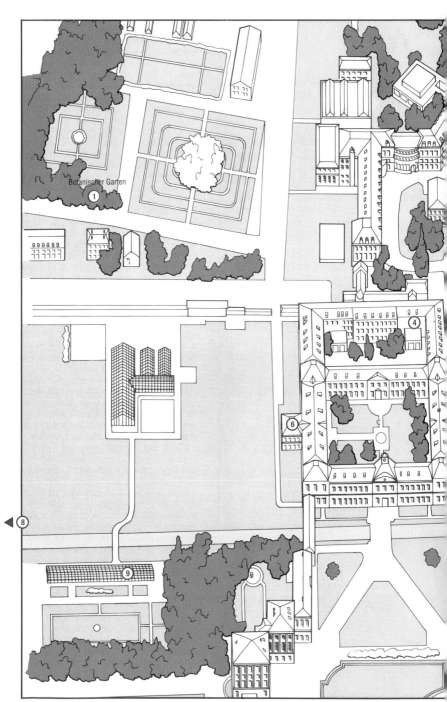

Botanischer Garten

▼40

# Nymphenburg (North)

A 20-minute tram ride (No. 12) from the Hauptbahnhof brings you to the outlying suburb of Nymphenburg. The main attraction here is the spectacular Nymphenburg Palace (Schloss Nymphenburg), the Versailles of Bavaria, with its vast, geometrical gardens and pagoda-dotted parkland. However, there is plenty to be seen outside the palace walls, most notably ① the **Botanic Gardens** (open daily 9 am-6 pm, entry 3 DM). The style here is subdued rather than showy, with neatly-ordered little clumps of flowers rather than gaudy riots. Walk west along Menzinger Strasse and you can take a ten-minute bus ride (route 73) to the lovely convent of Schloss Blutenburg. It comes as quite a shock to encounter ② the **Dreifaltigkeitskirche**, with its bizarre, umbrella-shaped roof, in such a quiet street as Maria-Ward-Strasse. ③ An antidote to the formal layout of the Nymphenburg is the charming little **Alter Nymphenburg Friedhof** (Old Nymphenburg Cemetery). ④ Of all the things you might expect to find in one of the palace outhouses, the university's **Genetics and Microbiology Department** is not one of them. ⑤ A vast semi-circular lawn, known as the **Schlossrondel**, faces the Nymphenburg Palace proper. Sited on its edge, with scrupulous symmetry, stand ten yellow houses built between 1728 and 1758 to accommodate the officers of the palace garrison and the workers at the Nymphenburg Porcelain Factory (founded 1747). ⑥ The **Museum of Mankind and Nature** (Museum Mensch und Natur): hard going on the ground floor, which is all minerals, but more interesting upstairs, when animals and human beings start getting involved. ⑦ Squeezed inside the tiny **Johannes Brunnenhaus** is the monstrous pumping machine that operates the fountain at the front of the palace. ⑧ Off the map in a wooded spot stands the **Magdalenenklause** (Magdalene Hermitage), built between 1725 and 1728 as a place of meditation for the Prince Elector Max Emanuel. In order to foster the illusion of rustic seclusion, the exterior has been constructed to look like a ruin. Similarly, the interior is half cave, half chapel. ⑨ The first of three elegant **hothouses** (1807-1820). The one furthest away from the palace, known as the Palmenhaus, has been converted into a lovely café-restaurant. Remember, though, that blue tablecloths denote self-service, while white linen tablecloths mean waitress service.

▼41

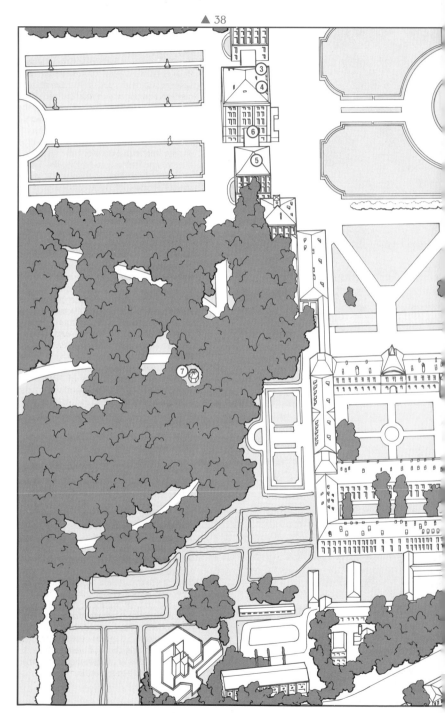

# Nymphenburg (South)

① A glorious, tree-lined **canal drive**, leading the eye and the visitor to the Nymphenburg Palace. ② From out of a seemingly haphazard pile of rocks, a **foaming banner of water** rises 30 feet in the air: all part of the skilful merger of nature and artifice that makes this one of the finest baroque complexes in Europe. It all began in 1662, when to celebrate the birth of their son Max Emanuel, Prince Elector Ferdinand Maria ordered work to begin on a summer villa for his Italian wife Henrietta Adelaide. From its inception, Nymphenburg was intended as a source of delight, but the Prince Elector's heart went out of the place when in 1676 Henrietta died aged 42. Little work was done until their son Max Emanuel started taking an interest in 1702, and from then on, Munich's rulers added to the site for 150 years. It is worth buying an all-in-one ticket (*Gesamtkarte*, 6 DM) that will admit you to all the Nymphenburg sights. ③ The first of these is the royal residence. You climb an imposing white staircase and find yourself in ④ the marvellous **Steinerner Saal** (Stone Room) banqueting hall, gazing up at frescos painted by Johann Zimmerman (1756). Other highlights are the **fireplace** in Room 2, the **back bedroom** (Room 12). ⑤ The most crowded room is **King Ludwig's Hall of Beauties** (Schönheitgalerie), hung with the portraits of 36 women who either were - or he wished were - his mistresses. Among them is raven-haired dancer Lola Montez, who cost Ludwig his crown: scandalized citizens forced him to deport her (she was 32 years younger than him), and he abdicated in protest. ⑥ Looking through the **archways** under the palace, you have an uninterrupted view down to the waterfall at the end of the gardens, more than a mile away. Of the many lovely garden houses that dot the grounds, the least adorned but by no means the least charming is ⑦ the wooden **summer pavilion**, part Turkish mosque, part Russian summer-house. Further on into the grounds are the exquisite little Amalienburg - a rococo hunting lodge - and the extraordinary Badenburg, with its sunken swimming pool. Also an oriental-style tea pavilion, the Pagodenburg. ⑧ Not to be missed is the **Marstallmuseum** (Carriage Museum) where you can see the crazed, nymph- and cherub-encrusted gold conveyances in which `mad' King Ludwig II (ruled 1864-86) rode. For details of all Nymphenburg opening times, telephone 179080.

SÜDLICHES SCHLOSSRONDELL

ROMANSTRASSE

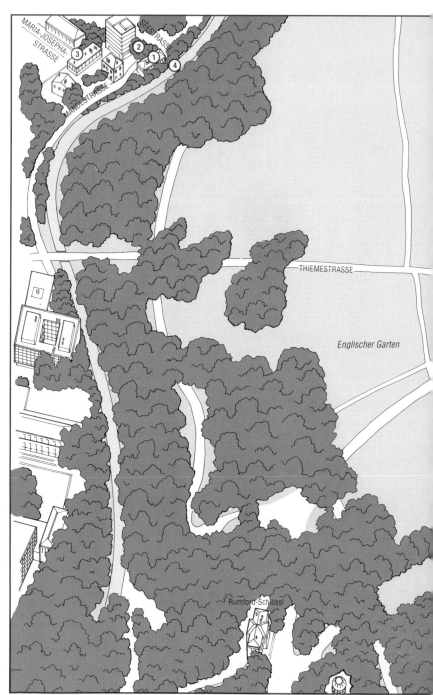

▼ 44

# Englischer Garten (North)

In the north-west corner of the Englischer Garten (*see pages 45, 55, 57 and 67*), the trees start to reach their branches into the back gardens of some of the city's most expensive and desirable houses. ① The impressive, classical **villa** in Mandlstrasse, just by the park entrance, is a notable example. ② Across the road, on the corner of Seestrasse, is a beautifully proportioned **house**. Note the delicate statue of a winged Hermes balancing in a scalloped first-floor alcove. The tone of the area is maintained by ③ No. 5 Mandlstrasse, where the centenary of **Thüga (Thüringer Gas) AG** is commemorated by an ambitious set of bronze doors. ④ A lovely little **bridge** leads from the street into the Englischer Garten proper. ⑤ The **Kleinhesseloher See**, an artificial lake (boating), beside which you can drink beer and put the children on a roundabout. Further to the east, the River Isar adjoins the park, and officially-sanctioned nude sunbathing takes place on its shores. To the north, the Englischer Garten extends another two miles (3 km), becoming less and less populated by pedestrians, although cyclists and (in winter) cross-country skiers still abound. Other delightful beer gardens can be found at Hirschau and Aumeister on the west bank of the Isar, and Emmeramsmühle on the east. ⑥ Broad open spaces of **parkland**, so large that people can set up picnics, volleyball courts, even whole football pitches and still not impinge on others. ⑦ A **children's playground**, with a thoughtfully-placed beer kiosk for parents. Little girls and boys tend to travel in style through the Englischer Garten, conveyed in small sidecars that are attached to their parents' bicycles. Tall, orange plastic flags announce their presence to other road users. ⑧ The pretty **Oberstjägermeister** brook winds through woods alive with wild garlic. ⑨ One **road** travels through the Englischer Garten, open to buses and bicycles but not to cars. There is only one bus stop in the park - at the Chinese Tower - and at this point foot-weary promenaders are further away from it than they are from the exit.

▼ 45

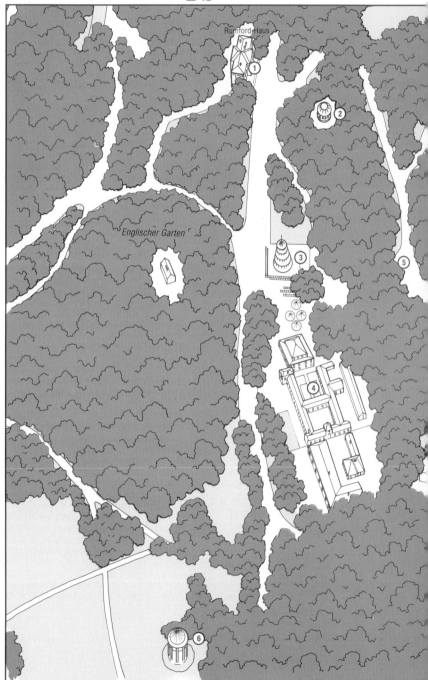

Rumford-Haus

Englischer Garten

# Englischer Garten (Centre)

① The pretty little **Rumford House**, built in 1791 by Johann Lechner as a tribute to the Englischer Garten's creator Count von Rumford (*see pages 55, 67*). The house originally served as an officers' mess, but is used today as a kindergarten. ② A beautiful little **merry-go-round**, constructed by Joseph Erlacher in 1913. Children ride on miniature state coaches, winter sleighs and galloping elks, to the jolly sound of an automatic barrel organ. ③ Centrepiece of this whole urban playground is the **Chinesischer Turm** (Chinese Tower), modelled on William Chambers' pagoda in London's Kew Gardens. Although burnt to the ground during an Allied bombing raid in 1944, the rickety wooden edifice has been rebuilt, and forms the focal point of the city's most famous beer garden. On a Sunday, the green tables around the tower can accommodate some 7,000 drinkers, munching their frisbee-sized pretzels, blowing froth off the top of their glasses and swaying in time to the Bavarian brass band that plays from the Chinesischer Turm's balcony. The beer is served from directly below the band's feet. No barrels are visible, giving the impression that the liquid is drawn up from subterranean springs. There is always a small queue, but it moves quickly - full glasses (*Radls*) are always waiting on the counter. The atmosphere at the Chinesischer Turm is informal, the dress casual to scruffy. The brew-quaffers squash together rather jovially on the communal tables, anarchists pressed up against bankers, the leather jackets of heavy metal fans rubbing up against the pullovers of librarians. ④ The **Okonomiehof** (1790) is a neat little single-storey complex, built to house the administrative offices for the park (as they still do today). As well as providing a place for people to promenade, the Englischer Garten served originally both as an agricultural college and a model farm. ⑤ Just by the Chinese Tower is the number 54 **bus stop**, a welcome sight to those for whom walking home is either unappealing or impossible. ⑥ Atop an artificial mound stands the **Monopteros**, a slender stone temple which has served as landmark and meeting place for one and a half centuries. In the 1960s, it was a gathering point for alternative thinkers and musicians alike; many still come to pay homage. The present structure was designed by Leo von Klenze in 1838, replacing the original, somewhat smaller wooden temple to Apollo.

HIRSCHAUER STRASSE

TIVOLISTRASSE

LERCHENFELDSTRASSE

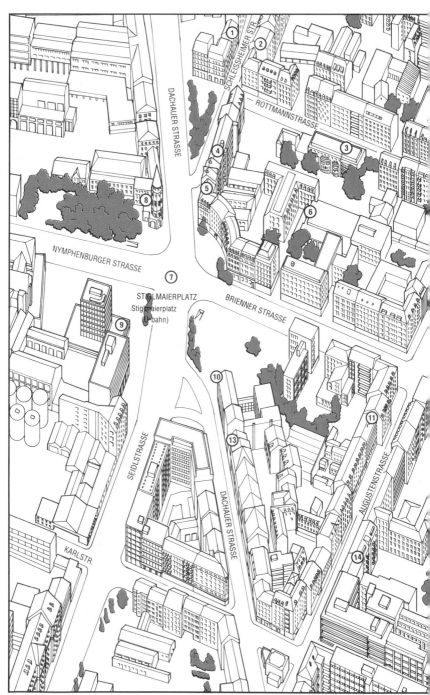

STIGLMAIERPLATZ
Stiglmaierplatz
(U-bahn)

DACHAUER STRASSE

SCHLEISSHEIMER STR.

ROTTMANNSTRASSE

NYMPHENBURGER STRASSE

BRIENNER STRASSE

SEIDLSTRASSE

DACHAUER STRASSE

AUGUSTENSTRASSE

KARLSTR.

▼ 58

# Stiglmaierplatz

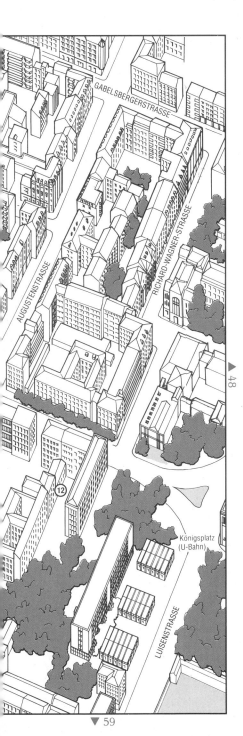

① The **Indienmarkt** grocery is thick with the scent of the sub-continent's herbs and spices. Oriental food shops are not common in Munich. ② **China Imbiss**, usually packed with Chinese people, a convenient little spot for a quick noodle dish (**D**). ③ The stylish **Neues Rottmann** cinema, architecturally distinguished by three statues protruding from its frontage: one woman holds a mask of tragedy, another a mask of comedy, while between them stands a helmeted torch-bearer. ④ An unusual billiard hall - a luminous, sea-green place - with the comfortable café **Philoma** at the front. ⑤ Next door is **Galerie M**, a novelty furniture shop where you can find denim sofas, zip-up wardrobes and a tiny red light which scampers across the floor like a crab. ⑥ It is easy to miss the **Münchner Volkstheater**, which is set back quite a way from the street, its presence announced only by two red and white poles and a small banner. The Volkstheater's logo is a girl riding a crocodile, and this fringe venue has a reputation for putting on plays with similar bite. ⑦ **Stiglmaierplatz** is the capital of the world-famous Löwenbräu empire. Its palace and pleasure grounds are housed within the imposing walls of ⑧ the **Löwenbräukeller**, not a cellar at all but a green-towered, pastel-frescoed complex with a warren of cosy drinking nooks off the rather grand and civilized main hall. The Löwenbräu brewery stands across the road. ⑨ Embedded in the walls of **Franz Mayer's** glass and mosaic factory are some of the company's more exotic samples. It's worth slipping into the courtyard to see their lovely stained glass windows. ⑩ The windows at **Werkhalle Bulthaup** are covered with a cage, except for one small patch: sneak a look at the space-age kitchens behind. Shelves are suspended by wires from the ceiling; tables are huge ring-binder folders with giant crayons for legs. ⑪ **Da Enzo**, a snug, light-blue painted pizzeria (**D**), with an attractive sandy interior. ⑫ The **Hansa Haus** is an attractive little beer garden at the back of No. 39 Briennerstrasse, overlooked by flats. ⑬ School buses are forever parked in long lines outside the **Münchner Theater für Kinder** (Munich Theatre for Children), which stages lavish productions throughout the day. ⑭ **'s Pfandel** (**D**) offers an interesting menu of Persian food, with imaginative vegetable dishes.

RICHARD-WAGNER-STRASSE

LUISENSTRASSE

ARCISSTRASSE

Königsplatz
(U-Bahn)

KÖNIGSPLATZ

MEISERSTRASSE

BRIENNER STRASSE

# Alte Pinakothek

An impressive brown and gold address plaque announces that No. 36 Gabels-bergerstrasse is the home of ① **Kanzler**, a dark and atmospheric second-hand book-shop. It serves the needs of the students who attend the university science faculties that are situated in this area. ② The **Hugo Ruef** auction house puts on four sales a year, usually an interesting mixture of the grand and the bizarre. ③ The **University of Technology** (1868). ④ An unexpected expanse of parkland is a suitably lush pre-lude to the **Alte Pinakothek**, the grandfa-ther of all art galleries. Built by Leo von Klenze between 1826 and 1836, it is a building on a grand scale, with paintings of similarly epic proportions (witness the Rubens rooms on the upper floor). It con-tains works by all the great European artists of the 14th to 18thCs, and although only two of its floors are open to the public, these are so vast as to defeat all but the hardiest aesthetes. If you have to choose one section at the expense of all others, try Rooms 5 to 13 on the upper floor. This will give you Rembrandt, Rubens, Van Dyck, Raphael, El Greco and Titian. Many visitors to Munich reserve a whole day for a trip to the Alte and Neue Pinakothek (*see pages 51, 89*): a good idea, but not on a Monday, when both are closed. ⑤ One of the city's grandest sights is the monumen-tal **Königsplatz**, a gigantic expanse of open ground, across which a collection of mon-umental, neo-classical buildings stare at each other. ⑥ Once the home of the soci-ety portrait painter Franz von Lenbach (1836-1904), the **Lenbachhaus** now dis-plays a collection of German art from prim-itive times to the modern day. The visitor can trace how the turn-of-the-century Ger-man art nouveau movement (*Jugendstil*) gave way to the more abstract, iconoclas-tic work of the Blaue Reiter (Blue Rider) group, which included Kandinsky and Klee. The oldest building on Königsplatz is ⑦ the **Glyptothek**, a mock Greek temple, built by Leo von Klenze between 1816 and 1830 to house his monarch King Ludwig I's col-lection of Greek and Roman sculpture. These plus more pieces are still on show. Next to go up was ⑧ a Corinthian-columned exhibition hall, now the **State Collection of Antiquities** (jewellery, glass and vases). ⑨ The **Propyläen** (1862), a purely ceremonial gateway, faces ⑩ the **State High School for Music**, once Hitler's *Führerbau*, where the Munich Agreement of 1938 was signed.

50

▼ 61

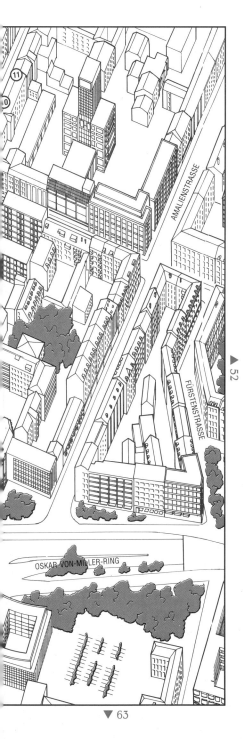

OSKAR-VON-MILLER-RING

AMALIENSTRASSE

FÜRSTENSTRASSE

▲ 52

▼ 63

# Theresienstrasse

① Not to be missed is the **Neue Pinakothek** (just off the map), a sandstone-coloured, skilfully-designed modern museum (1981) full of naturally-lit 18th and 19thC master-pieces both on canvas (Cézanne, David, Monet, Gauguin, Klimt, Van Gogh) and in bronze (Degas, Rodin). Exhibits are cleverly distributed through 22 rooms, covering some 11,500 square metres and revolving around two inner courtyards. The museum's moatside café is a good place to refuel with cake and coffee. As you munch, you can admire Henry Moore's large but graceful statue of a woman bathing. More challenging to picnickers is Moore's abstract ② *Die Liegende* (Reclin-ing Figures, 1970) on the other side of Theresienstrasse. These kidney-shaped visions stand in the parkland behind ③ the **Alte Pinakothek** (*see pages 49, 89*), one of the world's finest art collections. Three buildings supported by matchsticks stand in a line along ④ **Theresienstrasse**, and are home to a variety of university depart-ments, among them mineralogy, geology, meteorology, mathematics and paleontol-ogy. ⑤ Across the road is the **Pro Perkus-sion Center**, where everything on sale makes a noise, from *maraccas* to ten-piece drum kits. ⑥ **Alte Graphik** offers mustier pleasures, selling old Bavarian rural prints and lovely letter openers adorned with brightly-painted ducks. ⑦ An interesting lit-tle **arcade**, set back from the road and con-taining the **Birke** organic health food shop and two antiquarian bookshops, **S.B.** and **Maslowski**. ⑧ **Futon Futon**, selling colourful Japanese bedding and materials. ⑨ **Delphi II**, painted sky blue and white, offers cheap Greek food, long tables and nightly live *bouzouki* music (**DD**). ⑩ **Monika Schmidt's** gallery is a place to which antique map and print-seekers find their way in large num-bers. ⑪ The next-door **Dieter Frank** gallery is an altogether quirkier antiques empo-rium, where you are just as likely to pick up a modern naïve painting as an 18thC *chaise-longue*. ⑫ **Allotria**, a well-known jazz and rock venue. Its doors do not open until 8 pm: it takes its late-night ambience seri-ously. Liquids are the business of ⑬ the old-world **Pachmayr** store. Here you can buy 50 varieties of beer, some in tiny, col-lectable bottles, as well as a score of dif-ferent mineral waters and fruit juices. ⑭ A martyr to the motor car, **St Mark's Church** presides over a particularly busy stretch of ring road.

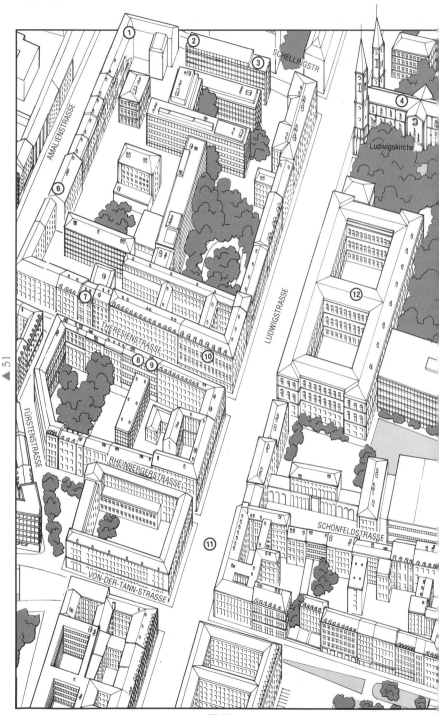

# University

Student haunts jostle against each other in this part of town. ① **Gaststätte Atzinger (D)** is one of the most popular, serving roast pork and potatoes for just 10 DM. The sustenance is literary at ② the **Anglia English Bookshop**, a seemingly chaotic repository of English-language publications. However, despite the seeming disorder, the staff all know exactly where each book is to be found. Next door ③ the cramped and crowded **Heinrich Frank University Bookshop** is packed from floor to ceiling with the slimline, yellow-covered Philip Reclam editions of major works, the prices astonishingly low because of the tininess of the print. ④ Colossal doors make the **Ludwigskirche** (built 1829-44) a difficult church to get into; once inside, the highlight is undoubtedly the mural of *The Last Judgment*, by Romantic painter Peter von Cornelius. It covers an area of the chancel wall some 20 metres by 10 metres (60 by 36 feet), second only in size to Michelangelo's *Last Judgment*, in Rome's Sistine Chapel. ⑤ A sleek, modern building houses the **School of Philosophy** on its first, second and third floors, while incongruously accommodating the **Unicorn Pizzeria (D)** at ground level. ⑥ **Amalienmarkt**, a Turkish greengrocers with a lovely display of fresh green vegetables and ripe fruit. ⑦ **Kaltenbrunner** specialize in medieval locks and door handles. ⑧ **Ursula Jorde** deals in accessories for antique dolls: you can pick up tiny boots, pianos, kitchen scales and even a horse and cart. ⑨ **Ikonen Galerie** handle extremely grand and expensive Russian icons. ⑩ Few buildings in Munich are grimmer than the exterior of the **Bayerische Versicherungs Bank** offices, which stretch almost 100 metres (975 yards) up to the dramatic ⑪ **Ludwigstrasse**, monumental creation of Leo von Klenze and his successor Friedrich von Gärtner, between 1817 and 1850. Look north and you will see Gärtner's Siegestor (Victory Gate) marking the start of Ludwigstrasse. ⑫ Gärtner's gigantic **State Library** (1834-39), with more than five million books and manuscripts. This is the biggest university library in Germany. Entering it, you walk up a grand flight of pillared stairs, with small lions climbing up the brass handrail. It is a copy of the Scala dei Giganti, in the Doge's Palace in Venice. Confused newcomers are encouraged to watch a 15-minute video on how to make use of the library.

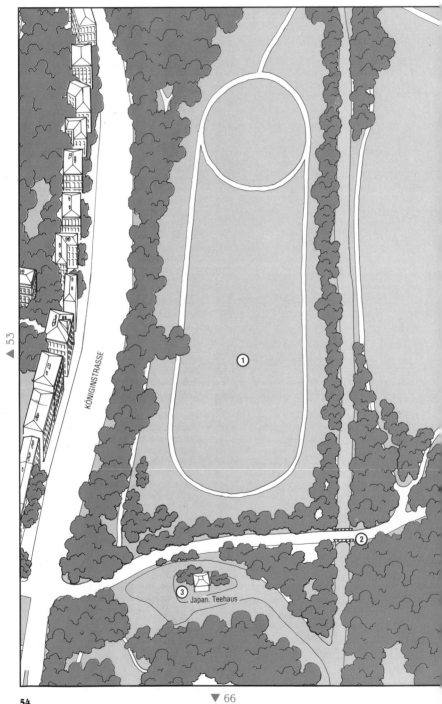

KÖNIGINSTRASSE

Japan. Teehaus

▼ 66

# Englischer Garten (South)

The Englischer Garten was the idea of a colourful expatriate American, Benjamin Thompson. In 1776, during the American War of Independence, Thompson's pro-British sympathies caused him to flee across the Atlantic. He took refuge in England, entered King George III's diplomatic service and was knighted in 1785. Seeking new adventures, he followed up an introduction to Bavaria's Elector Karl Theodor. Impressed, the Elector gave him a commission in the Bavarian Army. From this point on, Thompson's social stature grew as rapidly as did his fluency in the German language and familiarity with German ways. This was a time of dangerous social unrest, with soldiers having to keep a hungry populace in often brutal check. To defuse the tension, Thompson put forward a number of enlightened proposals. His first aim was to keep the poor content, which he did by setting up workshops and soup kitchens. His second aim was to keep the soldiers busy, by enrolling them in newly-founded schools and by putting them to work on municipal building projects. A means of achieving both aims simultaneously was to employ the army to create a large public park, where people could amuse themselves harmlessly. Thompson chose as his site a large expanse of bog on the outskirts of town, three miles long and one mile wide. Whereas contemporary Bavarian taste favoured the geometric lines of French gardens, Thompson and his German colleague Ludwig von Sckell went for the wilder `natural' look pioneered by English landscape gardeners Capability Brown and William Chambers. Hence the name `Englischer' Garten. For his services to Bavaria, Thompson was made a count; he chose the title Count von Rumford, the name of his home town in New Hampshire (re-named Concord by the victorious American rebels). He died in 1814. ① In this **southern** stretch, people gather to play football, throw frisbees, practise martial arts or strum their guitars and blow their flutes. ② Here the little **River Eisbach** becomes a minor torrent: sometimes you can see people surf-boarding. Those in search of serenity gather at ③ the **Japanese Tea House**, an island pavilion donated by Japan to mark the 1972 Munich Olympics (open only 1 Apr-31 Oct). On Sat and Sun afternoons during this period you can take part (for 5 DM) in the elaborate traditional Japanese tea ceremony (tel. 224319 for details).

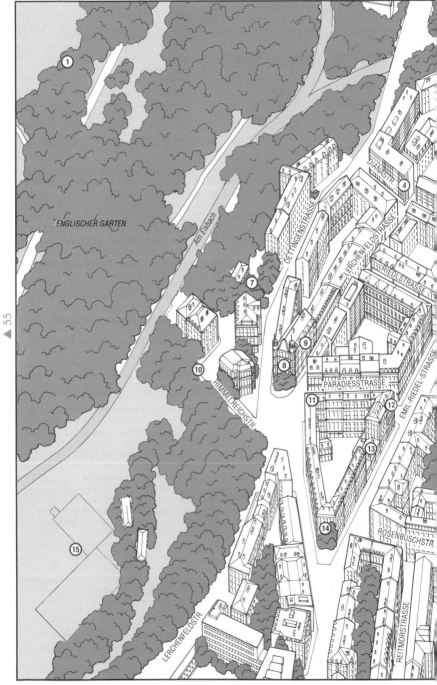

ENGLISCHER GARTEN

Am Eisbach

OETTINGENSTRASSE

DIANASTR.

LERCHENFELDSTRASSE

RIEDLSTRASSE

EMIL-RIEDEL-STRASSE

PARADIESSTRASSE

HIMMELREICHSTR.

ROSENBUSCHSTR.

REITMORSTRASSE

LERCHENFELDSTR.

# Oettingenstrasse

① These are the leafy **eastern fringes of the Englischer Garten**, within earshot of the frequent guitar and bongo-drum jamming sessions that go on beneath the park's peppermill-shaped gazebo, the Monopteros. ② A surprising little stretch of the **River Eisbach**, a tributary of the Isar. ③ **Palenque** serves Mexican food (**D**), but more interesting are the carvings on the outside of the restaurant. Beginning in Widenmayerstrasse and continuing round into Tivolistrasse, they depict the progressive ages and preocccupations of man and woman. ④ In the window of **W. Kraft**, you can watch a skilled upholsterer at work. ⑤ **Galerie Perlinger** sells exquisite gold ear-rings for 600 DM and more. ⑥ As Widenmayerstrasse becomes too wide and intimidating for a foot crossing, a **pedestrian tunnnel** offers escape to the sanctuary of the riverbank. ⑦ At the front of **No. 39 Oettingenstrasse**, rustic and green-shuttered, stands a little gatehouse in the same style; they contrast favourably with the somewhat soulless flats next door. ⑧ At the junction of three pretty little streets, an attractive **café-restaurant** (**D**) offers a leafy welcome to passengers descending from the No. 20 tram. ⑨ Cyclists stop for running repairs at the **Karl Griesbeck** cycle shop, which also sells new and second-hand bikes. ⑩ An unobtrusive **entry point** to the Englischer Garten. ⑪ Try the *Roggenbrot* (rye bread) at the little **Bäckerei Platzl**: the loaves are oval in shape, with markings like a gazelle. ⑫ The newly opened **Bat-Sing** chinese restaurant. ⑬ An old chair on top of a pole points the way into the rustic yard of **Bauernmöbel und Antiquitäten**. Here they restore desks and cupboards to the beautiful condition in which they sell them at their up-market shop next door (open Fridays, Saturdays only). ⑭ **Kanzleirat** (**DD**) offers shady tables, Bavarian grills and Yugoslavian specialities. ⑮ Amid the unkempt parkland of the Englischer Garten, this well-manicured municipal **sports field** looks suave and inviting in the extreme. ⑯ In the window to the left of the imposing office block at No. 38 Widenmayerstrasse, you may catch a glimpse of a flock of brightly coloured budgerigars, flying round their ground floor flat. ⑰ Three doors down, you may notice the pleasing **wrought-iron balconies** of No. 35. ⑱ Shady riverside **benches**, set back a welcome distance from the traffic.

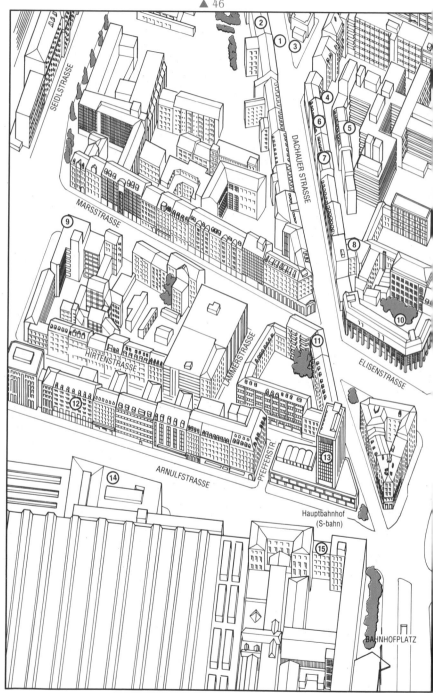

SEIDLSTRASSE

DACHAUER STRASSE

MARSSTRASSE

HIRTENSTRASSE

LÄMMERSTRASSE

ARNULFSTRASSE

PFEFFERSTR.

ELISENSTRASSE

Hauptbahnhof
(S-bahn)

BAHNHOFPLATZ

**58**

# Dachauer Strasse

① **Dachauer Strasse** leads northwest out of Munich, in the direction of the infamous Dachau concentration camp, 12 miles out of town. ② The window of **Army Shop** is a parade of military uniforms and equipment, ranging from thick socks and combat jackets to disembowelling knives and electric truncheons (brand name Liferider). ③ Sited here for no obvious reason, a pretty little statue of a Greek **Arion**, riding an evidently displeased dolphin. Behind No. 263 Dachauer Strasse stands a modern little courtyard, enlivened by ④ a huge mural of the city skyline and ⑤ the **Theater im Karlshof**, painted bright yellow and staging an imaginative range of shows, from farces to belly dancing, from cabaret to performance art. ⑥ Chocolate pianos, marzipan *Wurst* and oozing yoghurt and kiwi-fruit cakes are some of the attractions on display in the **Café Conditorei Bäckerei** at No. 24 Dachauer Strasse. ⑦ Speciality of the **Side Imbiss** (**D**) is pitta bread stuffed with cheese, aubergine and tomatoes. ⑧ Operating from a green and brown hut-like building behind No. 12 Dachauer Strasse, there is an establishment which sells a frightening array of handguns and rifles - with silencers. ⑨ At **Re-ell** kitchen showroom, each member of the sales staff has a kitchen for an office. ⑩ The vast glass and brick building at the bottom of Dachauer Strasse looks like a conference centre, but in fact it is the **Luisengymnasium** school. Its rear courtyard boasts interesting blue sculptures of domestic odds and ends. ⑪ **Zigarren Sommer** has a six-foot-high display of cigar boxes and pipes. ⑫ Amid the rather down-beat mass of station hotels, **Elisabeth Erhardt's** shop stands out; it sells every conceivable kind of religious carving, from airborne cherubs to kneeling saints. ⑬ Like a flash bulb perched upon a camera, the **Austrotel** soars above the station. ⑭ The northern wing of the Hauptbahnhof is known as the **Starnberger Bahnhof**. Trains leave from here for the Alpine ski resorts such as Garmisch-Partenkirchen. ⑮ Although attracting a somewhat seedy crowd on its fringes, the **Hauptbahnhof** has a light, airy feel to it, thanks to its cleverly suspended overhead walkways. Whereas in many international stations there is a sense of rush and desperation about their ticket-issuing areas, the Hauptbahnhof's *Reisezentrum* (travel centre) has the atmosphere of a leisurely reading room.

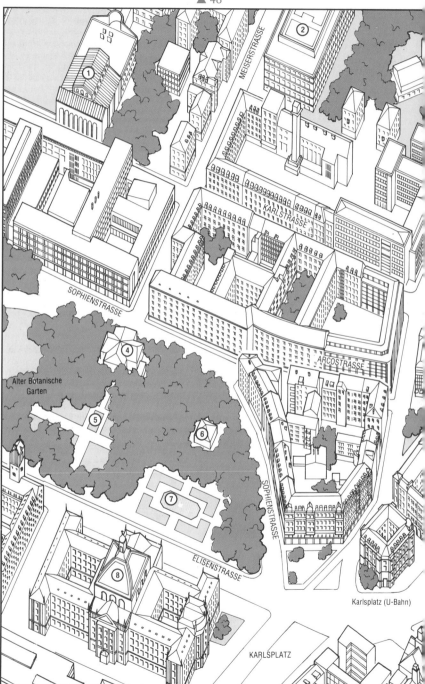

MEISERSTRASSE

KARLSTRASSE

SOPHIENSTRASSE

ARCOSTRASSE

Alter Botanische
Garten

SOPHIENSTRASSE

ELISENSTRASSE

Karlsplatz (U-Bahn)

KARLSPLATZ

# Karolinenplatz

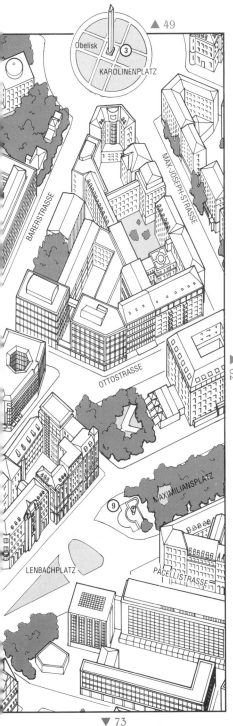

▲ 49

Obelisk

③

KAROLINENPLATZ

MAX-JOSEPH-STRASSE

BARERSTRASSE

▶ 62

OTTOSTRASSE

MAXIMILIANSPLATZ

⑨

LENBACHPLATZ

PACELLISTRASSE

▼ 73

① Unspectacular Karlstrasse is adorned by the unconventional **Basilica of St Boniface** (1835-50). Its towering central door carries a jumble of letters you have to piece together to read. Simpler to decipher is the right-hand door, which bears a Latin inscription saying 'The door to heaven' and at its top, some 20 feet (6 m) above, a crown and the words 'The home of God'. In between, two lions hover uncertainly. The basilica's interior is equally unusual, with circular pews. ② The **State Graphic Collection** is housed in the former administrative headquarters of the Nazi Party. The classically-styled building contains many thousands of woodcuts, copperplates and drawings, from the 14th to the 20thC, from Rembrandt to Hockney. You have to request the exhibits you want to see, and these are then brought to you in the Study Hall. Admission is free, and the collection is open Monday to Friday. ③ A spider's web of tram lines surrounds the giant **obelisk** in Karolinenplatz. This sombre monument commemorates the 30,000 Bavarians killed while fighting on Napoleon's side in the ill-fated 1812 campaign against Russia. ④ At night, the **Park-Café** is a club for the highly chic. By day it has a humbler role, serving beer and snacks from outdoor huts in ⑤ the **Alter Botanischer Garten** (Old Botanic Garden). This used to be the site of a giant glass palace, built in 1853 to house Germany's first-ever industrial exhibition. When the palace burnt down in 1931, the garden was turned into a public park. Much of the work was done by the architect Paul Troost, who also designed Hitler's Haus der Kunst, in Prinzregentenstrasse (*see page 67*). Here, his offering is more modest, in the form of ⑥ a little square **pavilion**, which these days puts on avant-garde art shows. ⑦ The **Neptune Fountain**, by contrast, is a giant structure, typical of the 1930s, featuring a very casual-looking Neptune striding over the backs of thrashing horses. Across the road rises the vast mass of ⑧ the **Justice Palace** (1897), built by Friedrich Thiersch. ⑨ Flanked on one side by a rearing horse, and on the other by a massive, thick-necked bull, the frothing **Wittelsbacher Fountain** is perhaps the most beautiful in the city (despite its traffic-beleaguered situation). It was constructed by Adolf von Hildebrand between 1893 and 1895, to commemorate the completion of a new municipal water supply system.

◀ 61

JÄGERSTRASSE

KARDINAL-DÖPFNER-STRASSE

FINKENSTRASSE

WITTELSBACHER-PLATZ

AMIRAPLATZ

BRIENNER STRASSE

SALVATORPLATZ

THEATINERSTRASSE

SALVATORSTRASSE

▶ 64

# Maximiliansplatz

① The modern **Bayerische Landesbank** building forms a blue-grey glass amphitheatre. ② **Harry's** sells vivid menswear, orange suits a speciality. A hundred yards away, two very different statues face each other across Ottostrasse. ③ Outside the otherwise sober offices of the **Süddeutsche Bodenkreditbank**, a naked young ponytailed girl pours water from a large jug. ④ Over the road, two giant concrete slabs entomb four soldiers' helmets as a **memorial** to the dead of World War I. ⑤ Impressive on horseback, **Elector Maximilian I** (1597-1651) cuts a lone figure in the middle of von Klenze's rather uniformly elegant Wittelsbacher-Platz. ⑥ The **Ludwig-Ferdinand Palace** (1825) and ⑦ the **Arco-Zinneberg Palace** (1820) are both von Klenze's work. ⑧ A discreet white awning and a strip of mauve carpet are all that announce the presence of **Aubergine** (DDD), one of Germany's most expensive gourmet restaurants, considered by many critics to be the finest in the country. Chef-owner Eckart Witzigmann has been hailed as a `culinary messiah'. Venison with wild berries and pigeon cutlets with lentils are among the good news he brings. ⑨ **Maximiliansplatz** is a racetrack of a square. However, its leafy central reservation houses a number of interesting statues. ⑩ The absorbing **Siemens Museum** contains hundreds of pioneering inventions. ⑪ The tall, cramped **Salvatorkirche** is spiritual home to the city's Greek community. ⑫ Orchestral and vocal sounds waft out through the windows of the **State Singing and Music School**. ⑬ The slender **Hugendubel Bookshop**, a perfect example of how to fit modern premises into a historic, but inconveniently-shaped old building. Large numbers of foreign-language books are available. ⑭ For a century and a half, the imposing **Hotel Bayerische Hof** has dominated Promenadeplatz. Marble walls, stained glass windows, a roof-top swimming pool and a chandelier-hung restaurant are some of its grander features. ⑮ The **Dreifaltigkeitskirche** (Holy Trinity Church) was built between 1711 and 1718 in grateful thanks to the Almighty for sparing the city from rampaging Austrian troops in 1705, during the War of the Spanish Succession (1702-1713). The church was designed by Giovanni Antonio Viscardi; cupola and ceiling frescos by Cosmas Damian Asam. Dreifaltigkeitskirche was one of the few churches to be spared damage in World War II.

◄ 63

GALERIESTRASSE

LUDWIGSTRASSE

ODEONSPLATZ

1

5

4

3

6

9

8

7

Odeosnplatz
(S-Bahn)

THEATINERSTRASSE

12

11

HOFGARTENSTRASSE

13

VISCARDI
GASSE

14

15

RESIDENZSTRASSE

17

16

Residenzmuseum

19

18

MARSTALLPLATZ

# The Residenz and the Hofgarten

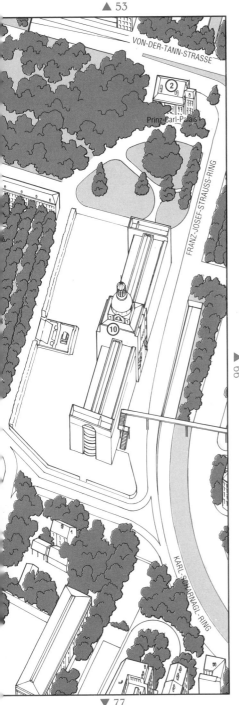

① The neo-classical **Leuchtenberg Palace** (Leo von Klenze, 1816-21), modelled on the Palazzo Farnese, in Rome. Now the Ministry of Finance. ② Next to a busy underpass stands the isolated **Prinz-Carl Palace** (1804-6) built by Klaus von Fischer for Ludwig I's brother Prince Carl. Today the Bavarian Prime Minister uses it for state receptions. ③ Striking **wall frescos** by Richard Seewald (1961), entitled *Ideal Landscapes*. ④ A **statue of Ludwig I** on horseback (1862) marks the middle of Odeonsplatz and the start of ⑤ the epic-scale **Ludwigstrasse.** ⑥ One of Munich's oldest cafes, the **Café Annast (D)**, beside which stand ⑦ colourful **wall frescos of Bavarian history**, painted by early 19thC artist Peter Cornelius. ⑧ The **Hofgarten** (1613-17), once the court vegetable garden, now an elegant public park. The centrepiece is ⑨ **Diana's temple**, a 12-sided green pavilion. ⑩ The domed shell of the **Bavarian Army Museum**, gutted in World War II. ⑪ The entrance to the Neuer Herkulessaal, now a concert hall but once the throne room of Ludwig I, stands to the east of the **State Collection of Egyptian Art** which forms the north-west tip of the vast Residenz complex, official residence of the Wittelsbach dynasty, who ruled Bavaria from 1180 to 1918. To the west of the Residenz soars the overwhelming, canary-yellow ⑫ **Theatinerkirche** (1622), built by Prince Elector Ferdinand Maria in thanks for the birth of his long-awaited son. ⑬ Stone lions guard the **Feldherrnhalle** (Hall of the Generals, 1841-44). Here Hitler's inflammatory procession of 9 November, 1923, ended in bloodshed: 14 Nazis and four policemen were shot dead, and Hitler was imprisoned for five years (but released after one). Under Nazi rule, all who passed by the Feldherrnhalle were required to give the Nazi salute. Many avoided the issue by taking ⑭ **Viscardigasse**, which became known as Drückerbergstrasse, or `Dodge-Down Alley'. ⑮ A glass or two in the long, elegant **Pfälzer Weinprobierstube** provides strength for a trip to the Residenz. Highlights are ⑯ the lovely, lozenge-shaped **Brunnenhof courtyard** (1610), ⑰ the ravishing red and gold **Cuvilliés-** (or Altes-Residenz) **theatre**, designed by the French dwarf François de Cuvilliés (1695-1768) and ⑱ the mind-boggling **Schatzkammer** (treasury).In addition, the **Residenz Museum** contains 112 splendid rooms. So vast is the complex that the tour is divided into morning and afternoon shifts. ⑲ **Entry** is via Max-Joseph-Platz.

▶ 66

VON-DER-TANN-STRASSE

Prinz-Carl-Palais

FRANZ-JOSEF-STRAUSS-RING

KARL-SCHARNAGL-RING

▼ 77

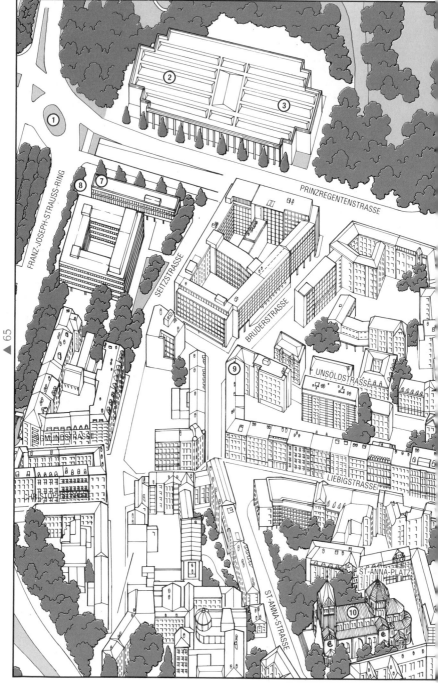

◄ 65

FRANZ-JOSEPH-STRAUSS-RING

PRINZREGENTENSTRASSE

SEITZSTRASSE

BRUDERSTRASSE

UNSÖLDSTRASSE

LIEBIGSTRASSE

GMUNDSTRASSE

CHRISTOP-STRASSE

ST-ANNA-STRASSE

ST-ANNA-PLATZ

# Prinzregentenstrasse

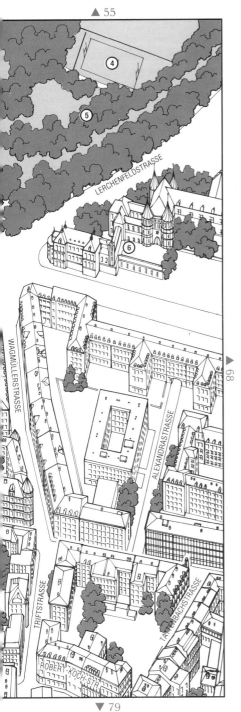

▲ 55

LERCHENFELDSTRASSE

WAGMÜLLERSTRASSE

ALEXANDRASTRASSE

TRIFTSTRASSE

TATTENBACHSTRASSE

ROBERT-KOCH-STR.

► 68

▼ 79

① A pedestrian-unfriendly intersection of main roads marks the beginning of the stately **Prinzregentenstrasse**, built between 1891 and 1907 in honour of the Prince Regent Luitpold I. This broad, busy avenue is known locally as 'Museum Mile', and ② at No. 1 Prinzregentenstrasse you find the many-pillared **State Gallery of Modern Art**, which houses priceless works by Dali, Matisse, Miro, Braque and the German Expressionists. The building was built during the Nazi era (by Paul Troost) and named Der Haus der deutschen Kunst (The House of German Art). At its opening in 1937, Hitler spoke out against 'un-German' art, and to illustrate his point staged two parallel exhibitions, one of confiscated 'degenerate' art, the other of selected State-approved works. Five times as many people came to see the 'un-German' show as came to see his exhibition of Nazi-vetted work. Today, many of the once-banned works - by Chagall, Kandinsky and others - are back on show. ③ In the eastern wing of the building is the **Haus der Kunst**, used for seasonal exhibitions such as the autumn **Grosse Kunstausstellung**, at which hundreds of Munich artists display and sell their work. ④ A little **playground** in the south-east corner of the Englischer Garten offers swings, a five-a-side football pitch and fixed, stone table tennis tables. Suitably it is within view of the ⑤ **Rumford Monument**, a tribute to Benjamin Thompson (Count von Rumford), the American philanthropist who created the Englischer Garten (*see pages 43, 45, 55, 57*). The inscription describes him as *Menschenfreunde* - 'People's Friend'. ⑥ The **Neue Sammlung** (New Collection) is the name for the State Museum for Applied Art, a design museum exhibiting everything from chairs to transistor radios, from posters to crash helmets. ⑦ The **Café zur Schönen Müncherin** has large numbers of tables, views of the Haus der Kunst and ⑧ an almost surreally frivolous little **fountain**, shaped like a trough, whose sole function is to spill water on to the pavement. ⑨ The grim, grey exterior of the **Pension Beim Haus der Kunst**, known for its vast breakfasts, is a suitably old-world introduction to the charming Lehel district, full of elegant buildings dating from Munich's great period of expansion (Die Gründerzeit) in the 1870s. ⑩ Faded **Pfarrkirche St Anna** (St Anna's Parish Church, 1887-92) is the Lehel's focal point. Its angel-thronged porch is a visual delight.

◄ 67

LERCHENFELDSTRASSE

SEEAUSTRASSE

CRUSIUSSTR

HIMBSELSTR

REITMORSTRASSE

AM GRIES

PRINZREGENTENSTRASSE

OETTINGENSTRASSE

WIDENMAYERSTRASSE

LIEBIGSTRASSE

STERNSTRASSE

# Prinzregentenbrücke or Luitpold Bridge

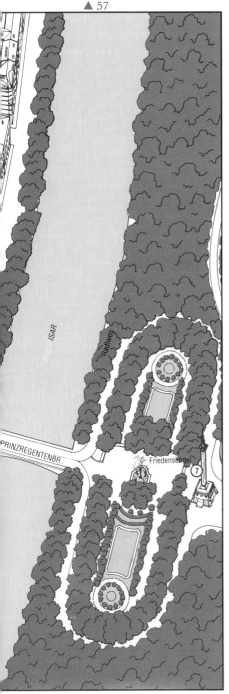

① **Marazzi**, a stylish little shop selling tiles with extravagant designs. ② What looks like a cluster of rust-coloured shipping containers piled on top of each other turns out to be the **State Prehistoric Collection** (1977), a record of life and times in Bavaria from the Stone Age to the early Middle Ages. ③ The **Bavarian National Museum** (1893-1900) takes over where its prehistoric partner leaves off. On show are 25,000 examples of Bavarian creativity, in the form of glass, jewels, clocks, furniture and porcelain. Architect Gabriel von Seidl wanted exhibits to match the building, so the museum is a carefully planned mixture of Renaissance, Romanesque, rococo, baroque and Gothic architectural styles. Highlights are the large Wessobrunn Room, just right of the entrance, with its valuable medieval ivories; room 16, containing carvings and sculpture by one 15thC artist, Tilman Riemenschneider; the stained glass display on the second floor; and the Christmas cribs in the basement. ④ Plenty of pictures of lazy, poppystrewn country afternoons at the **Schack Gallery**, the collection of 19thC romantic paintings assembled by art patron Adolf Friedrich, Count von Schack. If nothing else, do see Lenbach's *The Shepherd Boy*. ⑤ On a charmless patch of pavement stands a charming **fountain** depicting a merman and mermaid holding up their newlyborn child to be washed by jets of water. ⑥ **Luitpold Bridge** is guarded by four reclining figures, two male, two female, each one representing the areas ruled by the Bavarian royal family, the Wittelsbachs. The bridge was a present to the Prince Regent Luitpold on his 70th birthday in 1891. He had assumed power in 1886 after his mad nephew Ludwig II, Wagner-worshipping creator of the famous `fairytale' castles, drowned in a boating accident. ⑦ The golden **Friedensengel** (Angel of Peace) stands on top of a 23-metre (75-foot) column that soars out of a little Athenian-style temple held up by Greek maidens. She was created to mark 25 years of peace, following the defeat of the French (1871) in the Franco-Prussian War. Continue east down Prinzregentenstrasse and you come to the Roman-style Villa Stuck art gallery, the stupendous Feinkost-Käfer delicatessen and the beautiful Prinzregententheater (1901). ⑧ **Restaurant Sabitzer** (DDD) offers an elegant gold and white interior, and super-rich food. Open till 1 am.

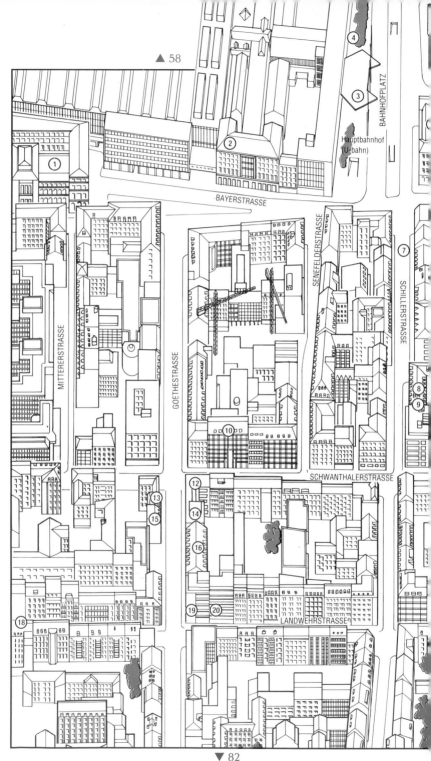

BAHNHOFPLATZ

Hauptbahnhof
(U-bahn)

BAYERSTRASSE

SENEFELDERSTRASSE

SCHILLERSTRASSE

MITTERERSTRASSE

GOETHESTRASSE

SCHWANTHALERSTRASSE

LANDWEHRSTRASSE

1

2

3

4

7

8

9

10

12

13

14

15

16

18

19

20

# Hauptbahnhof

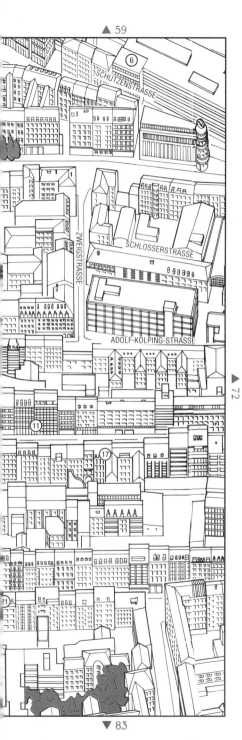

▲ 59

▶ 72

▼ 83

① The grimy **Bayerstrasse Post Office**, not to be confused with its open-all-hours brother in Bahnhofplatz. ② Beneath a wooden ceiling, an air of leafy calm prevails in the Hauptbahnhof **tourist information centre**. ③ A florist's, housed under a transparent suspended ceiling, sets the stylish tone for the **Hauptbahnhof**, built and rebuilt many times since 1840. ④ At the **Deutsche Verkehrs-Kredit-Bank,** you can change money from 6 am to 11.30 pm. At ⑤ the **Central Post Office**, you can change money at any time of night or day. ⑥ **Hertie** is the longest department store in Munich; its basement houses the Käfer delicatessen, suppliers to the very smartest. ⑦ **Schiller-strasse** is typical of the streets immediately round the station: cheap hotels, quick food, Turkish and Yugoslavian electrical shops plus some very sleazy sex joints. To avoid confusion, you should check the orientation of the clientele that the bars cater for. At No. 11a Schillerstrasse, for example, ⑧ the **Dolly Bar** has girls on show, while the artistes next-door at ⑨ **Cabaret Broadway** are transvestites. ⑩ Unusual for this area, an attractive hotel, the **Budapest**, with pale, coffee-coloured modern exterior and smoked-glass porch awning. ⑪ The **Aldi Supermarket**, one of the few fresh food places in this area. ⑫ The **Sultan (D)**, biggest and smartest of the many Turkish restaurants in the area. ⑬ **Diät Reformhaus**, a fresh green and yellow health food shop, an odd sight in such a bleary-eyed area. ⑭ The cramped **Çavusoglu Helal** supermarket, where piles of pitta bread dwarf the girl on the till. ⑮ **Weinstübe Schwarzwaldmädl**: a tired top hat and bottle of fake champagne stand in the window of this dimly-lit establishment. ⑯ **Kunsthandlung Rahmen-Mayr** sell small, colourful metal carvings showing shop scenes (butcher's, tailor's, dairy). ⑰ Home to all the big, Broadway-type musicals, the **Deutsches Theater**. ⑱ **Dimitra**, a sad little bridal shop. ⑲ Expatriate Turks crowd into the **Çavusoglu Imbiss**, no bigger than a cupboard, for kebabs at giveaway prices. ⑳ Outside the **Dolu** electrical goods shop, passers-by stop to stare at water pouring out of a tap which is somehow suspended in mid-air. Specialities at ㉑ the **Dubrovnik** Yugoslavian restaurant are goulash and Zagreb schnitzel filled with sheep's cheese and ham (**D**).

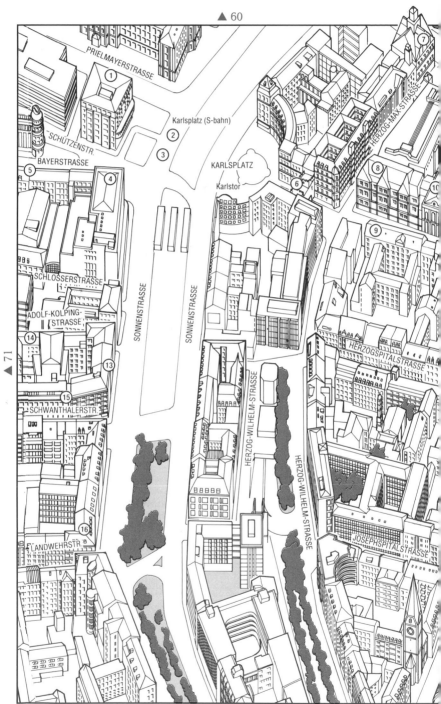

PRIELMAYERSTRASSE

SCHÜTZENSTR.

BAYERSTRASSE

SCHLOSSERSTRASSE

ADOLF-KOLPING-STRASSE

SCHWANTHALERSTR.

LANDWEHRSTR.

SONNENSTRASSE

SONNENSTRASSE

Karlsplatz (S-bahn)

KARLSPLATZ

Karlstor

HERZOG-MAX-STRASSE

HERZOGSPITALSTRASSE

HERZOG-WILHELM-STRASSE

HERZOG-WILHELM-STRASSE

JOSEPHSPITALSTRASSE

① ② ③ ④ ⑤ ⑥ ⑦ ⑧ ⑨ ⑩ ⑬ ⑭ ⑮ ⑯

# Karlsplatz

One of the main pleasures of eating at ① the super-gourmet **Hotel Konigshof (DDD)** is looking down on the traffic-devastated ② **Karlsplatz** and feeling glad you are not out there. Underground, things are better: ③ the Karlsplatz **subterranean shopping centre** is not an unpleasant place to stop for a stand-up beer and *Wurst* or, late at night, to pick up first editions of tomorrow's newspapers. This underground world also houses a tourist information centre, and it also gives direct access to the wonderful ④ **Kaufhof** department store food hall where you can buy delicious black-smoked Kapuziner ham. ⑤ The **Mathäser-Bierstadt** is the largest beer hall in the world, half palace, half dungeon. Focal point is the first floor music room, a vast arena with a Bavarian band in the middle. Giant pillars, giant coat hangers and giant glasses of beer brought to your table (cash on delivery). ⑥ **Karlstor** (Charles Gate, 1302) marks the start of the pedestrianized Neuhauserstrasse, Munich's biggest shopping street; look for the trio of child musicians in the gate archway. To the left of the gate stands the splashing Brunnenbuberl, or Little Boy Fountain, whose nudity caused a storm of protest when first unveiled in 1895. ⑦ Beleaguered by traffic, **Das Mövenpick (DD)** is a modern, eight-restaurant complex fitted into a 19thC house built as a meeting place for artists, known as the Künstlerhaus and decorated with grinning satyrs, voluptuous women and a maze of sub-floors and terraces. The orange awnings and plastic chairs outside are a definite mistake. ⑧ The frantic **Karstadt** department store, more down-market than Kaufhof, but more up-market than ⑨ **Kaufhalle**. ⑩ The **Bürgersaal** (1710) is a dazzlingly white church with an exhibition in its crypt commemorating Father Rupert Mayer, who died from injuries received in the concentration camp to which he was sent for preaching resistance to the Nazis. ⑪ The **Augustiner** restaurant **(DD)** and *Bierkeller* **(D)** have been serving hearty food and beer since 1897. ⑫ The **Richard Strauss Fountain** (1961) depicts frightening scenes from the composer's opera *Salome*. ⑬ Carry on down the passageway at No. 12 Sonnenstrasse, past the garish Sex-World, and you come to ⑭ two comfortable little cinemas, the **City** and the **Atelier**. ⑮ **Strudelhaus** sell home-made cherry, cheese and poppyseed strudels. ⑯ Visiting **Café Piccadilly** is a neon adventure. Go for the cocktails.

▶ 74

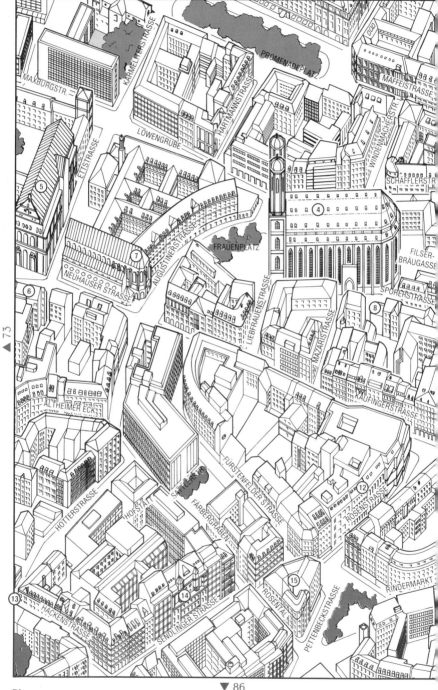

▲ 73

MAXBURGSTR.

KARMELITERSTRASSE

PROMENADEPLATZ

MAFFEISTRASSE

HARTMANNSTRASSE

WINDENMACHERSTR.

LÖWENGRUBE

ELISENSTRASSE

SCHAFFLERSTR

5

4

AUGUSTINERSTRASSE

FRAUENPLATZ

FILSER-
BRÄUGASSE

7

NEUHAUSER STRASSE

LIEBFRAUENSTRASSE

SPORERSTRASSE

6

8

MAZARISTRASSE

ALTHEIMER ECK

KAUFINGERSTRASSE

FÜRSTENFELDER STRASSE

12

HOTTERSTRASSE

HOFSTATT

SATTLERSTR.

FARBERGRABEN

ROSENSTRASSE

RINDERMARKT

15

13

14

ROSENTAL

HACKENSTRASSE

SENDLINGER STRASSE

PETTENBECKSTRASSE

# Marienplatz

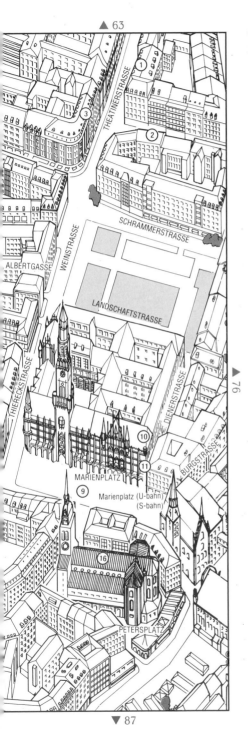

① The **Café Feldherrnhalle** owes its style and most of its clientele to an earlier era. ② The long-established **Franziskaner Restaurant (DD)** is both cheap enough for students and grand enough for post-opera parties. Beneath vaulted ceilings, one feasts on filling *Leberknödel* (soft liver dumpling) soup and *Spanferkel* (suckling pig). ③ Old-fashioned, excellent, pricy and fish-oriented: that is **Restaurant Boettner (DDD)**, one of Munich's top five since 1905. ④ The twin-domed towers (325 feet, 100 m high) of the magnificent **Frauenkirche** are used on a thousand guidebook covers. Building began in 1468. Make sure to take in the exquisitely carved C15th tomb of King Ludwig IV; also the multi-coloured modern pulpit (1957). A dent in the porch step is meant to have been made by the devil, gleeful that the choir windows had been forgotten by the architect. In fact they were just obscured by the high altar. ⑤ **St Michael's Church** (1597, Italian Renaissance), an elegant, grey edifice with a beautifully gabled façade, the model and inspiration for all Renaissance church architecture in southern Germany. ⑥ **Zum Pschorrbräu (D)** has a warm pink interior. ⑦ A wild boar stands guard outside the **German Museum of Hunting and Fishing.** ⑧ **Nürnberger Bratwurstglöckl am Dom**, a locals-packed place for *Wurst* **(D)**. ⑨ The real heart of town is **Marienplatz,** where jugglers, buskers, fast food and tourists meet. ⑩ The neo-Gothic **New Town Hall** (Neues Rathaus, 1867-1909) dominates the square: every morning at 11am and 9 pm the coloured figures in its clocktower act out various routines. In the centre of Marienplatz, look for the golden Mariensäule (Mary's Pillar), erected in 1632, and the C19th Fischbrunnen (Fish Fountain). Down in the Rathaus catacombs, ⑪ the **Ratskeller (DD)** serves tender *Kalbsbratwurst* and Salvator Bock, a dark, sweet powerful beer. ⑫ **Zum Spöckmeier** is *the* place for *Weisswurst*, Munich's soft white sausage, made with veal and herbs **(DD)**. ⑬ **Hundskugel** (1640), Munich's oldest restaurant, serving *Tafelspitz* (boiled beef) with horseradish (*meeretich*) that makes the nostrils sing. ⑭ The home of *Süddeutsche Zeitung* and its sister *Abendzeitung*. ⑮ Frescos decorate the upper floors of the triangular **Ruffini Houses.** ⑯ The mighty **St Peter's Church.** This is Munich's oldest church, dating back to 1368. Climb 300 steps up the tower for a spectacular view of the city and the Alps.

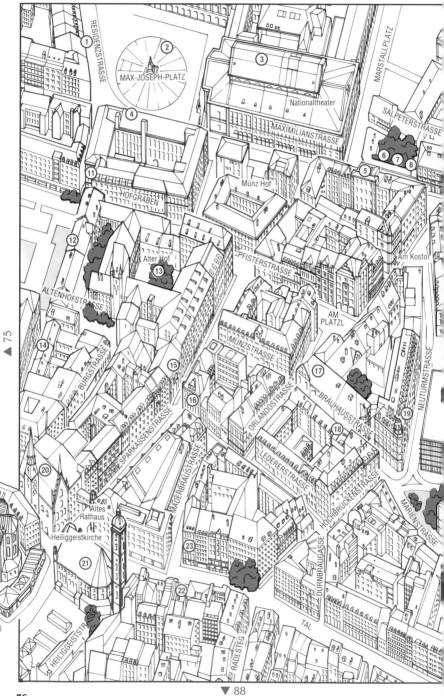

RESIDENZSTRASSE

MAX-JOSEPH-PLATZ

MARSTALLPLATZ

Nationaltheater

SALPETERSTRASSE

MAXIMILIANSTRASSE

Münz Hof

HOFGRABEN

Alter Hof

PFISTERSTRASSE

Am Kostor

ALTENHOFSTRASSE

AM PLATZL

MÜNZSTRASSE

BURGSTRASSE

ORLANDOSTRASSE

BRAUHAUSSTRASSE

NEUTURMSTRASSE

SPARKASSENSTRASSE

MADERBRÄUSTRASSE

LEDERERSTRASSE

HOCHBRÜCKENSTRASSE

MARIENSTRASSE

Altes Rathaus

Heiliggeistkirche

DÜRNBRAUGASSE

HEILIGGEISTSTRASSE

RADLSTEG

TAL

# Max-Joseph-Platz

① At **Spatenhaus**, the ground floor restaurant has an attractive, painted ceiling, the upstairs restaurant has smart, green walls and tablecloths. The speciality is the *Bayerischeplatte* of ham and suckling pig (**DD**). Diners look straight out on ② **Max-Joseph-Platz**, in the centre of which the first Bavarian king Max I Joseph (1799-1825) waves a cheery greeting. ③ Behind him rise the huge, white Corinthian columns of the **National Theatre** (1811, rebuilt 1825, 1963), next door to the New Residence Theatre. World famous for opera, it was here that Wagner launched *Tristan und Isolde*. ④ The red and yellow building on the south side of the square, formerly the Palais Törring-Jettenbach, is now the **Residenzstrasse Post Office** (1747). Going down Maximilianstrasse, the prices go up. ⑤ At **Kastl**, cocktail dresses go for 2,000 DM. Next door at ⑥ **Moshammer**, they don't even put the price on; the same goes for ⑦ jewellers **Hemmerle**. ⑧ **Gold Pfeil** handbags also cost 2,000 DM. ⑨ Epicentre of this prosperity is the **Hotel - Vier Jahreszeiten** (Four Seasons), Munich's top hotel for the past one and a half centuries. ⑩ A row of familiarly up-market shops (St Laurent, Louis Vuitton, Ralph Lauren) queue to serve the hotel guests. ⑪ **Wallach** specialize in Bavarian folk art and costume, still widely worn as Sunday best. ⑫ **Alois Dallmayr**, purveyors of luxury foods. ⑬ The courtyard of the **Alter Hof** (Old Court, 1255) is a tranquil spot. ⑭ **Strumpfhaus** sell tights and stockings. ⑮ **Zerwirkgewölbe** wild game (boar, venison, elk) and ⑯ **Haxnbauer Stuben** (**DD**) hams spitted and roasted on the premises. ⑰ The hearty **Hofbräuhaus** beer hall (1644), Munich's most famous drinking spot, is where, on 24 February 1920, an unknown political agitator called Adolf Hitler first addressed a large audience. ⑱ **Komödianten-Stadl** puts on the best Bavarian folk music show in Munich. ⑲ The grand white **Rafael Hotel** wants to wrest the title of best hotel in Munich from the Vier Jahrzeiten. ⑳ The neo-Gothic **Old Town Hall** (Altes Rathaus, 1470-80), reconstructed after a fire in 1460 and bombing in World War II. Look out for the ingenious wind chimes under the archway and check to see if its clock tells exactly the same time as the next-door ㉑ **Church of the Holy Ghost** (Heilig Geist); it should. ㉒ **Weisses Bräuhaus** serves lovely *Weissbier* in sedate, wood-panelled surroundings (**D**). ㉓ **Bogner im Tal** is a popular youthful hideaway and eating place (**D**).

78

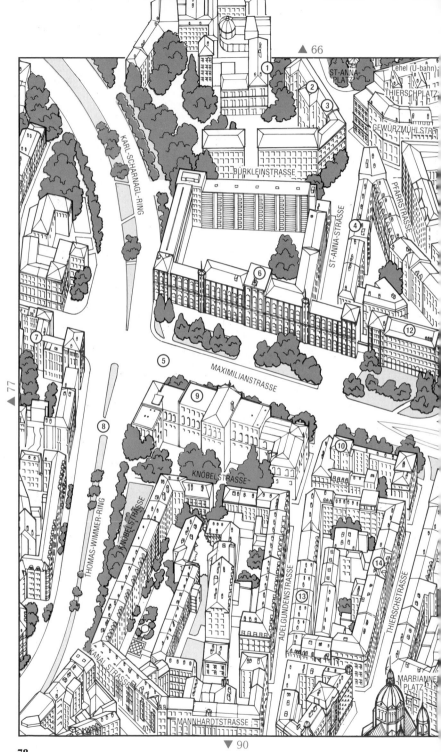

Lehel (U-bahn)

ST-ANNA-
PLATZ

THIERSCHPLATZ

GEWÜRZMÜHLSTR

BÜRKLEINSTRASSE

PFARRSTRASSE

ST-ANNA-STRASSE

KARL-SCHARNAGL-RING

MAXIMILIANSTRASSE

KNÖBELSTRASSE

KNÖBELSTRASSE

THOMAS-WIMMER-RING

ADELGUNDENSTRASSE

THIERSCHSTRASSE

MARRIANNE
PLATZ

KANAL-STRASSE

MANNHARDTSTRASSE

# Maximilianstrasse

① Badly damaged during World War II, the lovely little grey-and-white **St Anna im Lehel Klosterkirche** is now restored to its original glory. It was built between 1727 and 1733 by Johann Michael Fischer, who pioneered Bavarian rococo architecture. ② Next door is the elegant **Blumen Wildgruber** florist's shop, and two doors down the very proper ③ **Café Konditorei Wünsche** with high-backed chairs and old Munich atmosphere. No building in the city has a more elegant frontage than that of the tapering, charcoal and white ④ **Hotel Opera**. And no avenue is grander than ⑤ the prestigious **Maximilianstrasse**, built by Maximilian II, who came to the throne in 1848 after his father Ludwig I was forced to abdicate because of a scandalous love affair with the dancer Lola Montez. ⑥ The long, red building housing the **Upper Bavarian Administration** (Regierung von Oberbayern). Across the road, ⑦ a reminder of imperialism's dangers is the modest little **Jewish Museum** (Jüdisches Museum), with its photographs of pre-Nazi Munich Jewry and documents recording small, lost voices from the Holocaust (open Tues, Wed, Sun, afternoons only). ⑧ Avoid the racetrack-like **Thomas-Wimmer-Ring**, a roaring reproach to Munich's post-war town planners. Just as stentorian is the inscription above ⑨ the newly-scrubbed **Museum of Ethnology** (Museum für Völkerkunde). It reads: 'To My People The Honour and Glory' ('*Meinem Volk Zu Ehr Und Vorbild*'). ⑩ **No. 44, Drexler**, is an agonizingly exclusive boutique, its bare interior reinforcing the theory that the more expensive a shop is, the less stock it displays. Of the many statues in this street, the star is ⑪ **Maximilian II** himself. The tram lines part respectfully round the balding monarch, who has an uninterrupted view back up towards the city centre. Under his toes, four children are holding the coats of arms of the Bavarian territories (Bavaria, Swabia, Franconia and parts of the Rhineland Palatinate, or Pfalz). ⑫ To his right, the **Kleine Komödie** theatre, home of many a long-running farce. A cheap eating place in this up-market area is ⑬ the **Café Bistro Fragezeichen** (D), which crowds the pavement with blackboards advertising the day's specials. ⑭ **Villa Borgese**, an attractive piano bar and Italian restaurant (DD), with a lovely, statue-dotted walled garden at its rear.

STERNSTRASSE

RETTMORSTRASSE

ROBERT-KOCH-STRASSE

GEIBELZMÜLLERSTRASSE

WIDENMAYERSTRASSE

Pallas Athene

MAXIMILIANSBRÜCKE

MAX-PLANCK-STRASSE

Maximilianeum
(Bayer. Landta

① ② ③ ④ ⑤ ⑥ ⑦ ⑧ ⑨ ⑩ ⑪ ⑫

# Maximilianeum

① Entry to the quirky **Climax** restaurant (**D**) is via the narrowest of corridors, past the painfully aesthetic bar and down past a stage to a subterranean eating area peopled by odd wooden creatures. The food is lean and leafy, with occasional chicken breasts. More mainstream is ② the **Mühle im Lehel** (**D**), a cosy, net-curtained little local restaurant with yellow corn-ears hanging over the entrance and old-fashioned table lamps suspended over each table. ③ The **Skorpios** restaurant (**D**) serves excellent Greek bean soup. ④ **Tadora** is a gift shop so excruciatingly tasteful it is almost empty. It sells watches embedded in perspex and wine glasses with stems 20 cm long. ⑤ White tablecloths, white clapperboard walls and cheap food at **Pizzeria da Franco** (**D**). ⑥ The glowering headquarters of the **Bayerische Versicherungskammer** (Insurers' Confederation) present a grim exterior, apart from the attractive little bridge that links one block to another over the top of Gewürzmühlstrasse. The centrepiece is a gold clock, on one side of which a man reaps, while on the other a woman sows. ⑦ The elegant apartments along **Widenmayerstrasse** are protected by the river's stout-looking embankment walls, erected in 1893. Cyclists and, in winter, tobogganists abound in ⑧ the **Maximiliananlagen**. The most daring take advantage of a well-known and well-worn slope beneath the circular walls of ⑨ the **Maximilianeum**. Built by the educationally-minded Maximilian II (ruled 1848-64) as an educational establishment for the élite, it now houses the Bavarian parliament. A bold red edifice with golden frescos on its pediments, it looks immensely striking when viewed from a distance. From ⑩ the **Maximilian Bridge** (built 1903-5 by Friedrich von Thiersch), the view is spectacular. Downriver, in the distance, you can see the tower of the Volksbad baths; upriver the frothing waters of the Isar as it travels over a pair of gentle waterfalls. Lampposts rise along the bridge's parapet at regular intervals, except at one point, where instead of a lamppost there stands the imposing stone figure of ⑪ **Pallas Athene**, installed in 1906. ⑫ The island below the bridge is called the **Praterinsel**, on which stands the Anton Riemerschmid winery, founded in 1835.

Maximiliananlagen

MARIA-THERESIA-STRASSE

UNTERE FELDSTR.

BOGENSTR.

MAX-PLANCK-STRASSE

SCKELLSTR.

SCHILLERSTRASSE

GOETHESTRASSE

PETTENKOFERSTR.

LESSINGSTRASSE

NUSSBAUMST

BEETHOVENPLATZ

BEETHOVENSTRASSE

GOETHESTRASSE

# Pettenkoferstrasse

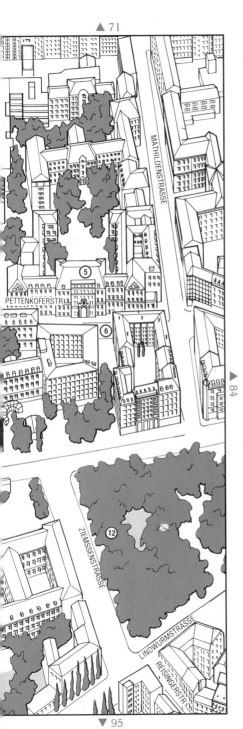

▶ 84

① The **Backhaus Bergbauer**, founded in 1907, is a café with its own bakery in the back. ② Next door, the **Goldener Anker** (**D**) is a large, homely establishment with pinewood booths and Yugoslavian elements to both its menu and its customers. Especially recommended is the *Schindelbraten* (pork chop platter). For afters you can visit ③ the **Café Bar Red Piano**, the louchest of dives, with thick, red drapes. ④ Cheap, but open only to holders of student cards, is the one-storey, green-tinted **Mensa** (**D**), where the area's many trainee nurses and doctors can choose from set menus at 5 DM and less. ⑤ Carvings of Asclepius and Hippocrates guard the towering frontage of the **Poliklinik** (General Clinic, 1863), centrepiece of the Ludwig-Maximilians-Universität (Ludwig Maximilians University) medical faculty. ⑥ **Pettenkoferstrasse** is named after the chemist Max von Pettenkofer (1818-1901), who preached the virtues of clean water in the fight against cholera and typhus. His grave is in the Old Southern Cemetery (Alter Südlicher Friedhof), his statue in Maximilansplatz (*see page 62*). ⑦ Many generations of surgeons have learnt their craft beneath the stern, grey dome of the **School of Anatomy**, the proceedings shielded from outside gaze by discreetly frosted windows. ⑧ The many-turreted, tree-shrouded hotel **Pension Mariandl** is a dark, woody excursion into a more elegant past. Ever-so-slightly faded, this tall, dignified establishment serves dinner and classical chamber music (**DD**) every weekday evening. ⑨ At the corner of **Lessingstrasse** and **Goethestrasse** stands one of the city's most characterful statues: a head-scarfed peasant woman, pausing from her work in the fields to mop her brow. It invests the pretty little **Beethovenplatz** ⑩ with an air of suburban serenity. ⑪ Housed in the basement of an impressively proportioned, five-storey, bright yellow town house, the **Goethe-Keller** (**DD**) is well-known for the adventurous sauces with which it adorns not just meat but vegetables too. ⑫ There is a shortage of leafy places to have a picnic in this part of Munich, but **St Matthew's Park** is a pleasant, woody little retreat, although you risk your life in raging traffic in order to get there.

SONNENSTRASSE

HERZOG-WILHELM-STRASSE

HERZOG-WILHELM-STRASSE

KREUZSTRASSE

SONNENSTRASSE

MATHILDENSTRASSE

PETTENKOFERSTRASSE

SENDLINGER-TOR-PLATZ

WALLSTR.

NUSSBAUMSTRASSE

Sendlinger Tor
(U-bahn)

LINDWURMSTRASSE

FLIEGENSTRASSE

THALKIRCHNER STRASSE

AUGSBURGERSTRASSE

PESTALOZZISTRASSE

REISINGERSTRASSE

STEPHANSPLATZ

# Sendlinger Strasse

① The **Mathilden-Bad** sauna, an establishment of almost clinical cleanness. Outside the Sonnenstrasse post office stands ② a somewhat plaintive **statue** of a man with pigeons on his shoulder. ③ **Sendlinger Tor** (first built 1318) was once part of the outer city wall. It once had three archways, replaced by the single large archway in 1906. It guards the entry to one of Munich's most variegated shopping streets, ④ the sinuous **Sendlinger Strasse**. ⑤ **Optik Paradies Suchy** stocks hundreds of pairs of spectacles, stylish and grotesque, novelty and antique. ⑥ Romantic-style coloured frescos adorn the frontage of the beautifully-restored **Singlspielerhaus**, once a brewery. Opposite stands ⑦ the fawn-coloured, delicately-carved frontage of the **Asam-Haus** (1733), home to the two Asam brothers Cosmas and Egid. Their house stands next to ⑧ the extraordinary church they built, dedicated to St Johann Nepomuk, but popularly known as the **Asamkirche** (1746), a South German baroque gem. Outside, the marble façade contains rough-hewn rocks and a statue of Johann Nepomuk, a Bavarian saint. Highlight of a dazzling interior is the towering two-tier altar, containing the saint's tomb. Behind the church is the strange little ⑨ **Asamhof Passage**, a new square with a compact disc shop, an eerily lit wall fountain, a *confiserie* selling chocolate beetles and a bizarre brick statue that is half man, half woman and has one outsize foot. ⑩ The **Sauter** camera shop stretches a full 60 metres along Sonnenstrasse. Behind it, in Pettenkoferstrasse, hides ⑪ the green-shuttered **Zum Bürgerhaus** (**DD**), built in 1827 and today offering cosy nooks, low lighting and high-quality food. ⑫ Trams slalom lithely round the flowerbeds on the surface of **Sendlinger Tor Square**, while in the rather jolly little underground shopping centre, people eat sausage and beer off wooden barrels. ⑬ **St Matthew's Church** (1955) has a bold, sweeping design, somewhat like a velodrome: the taller of its two towers can be seen for miles around, with its distinctive blue and gold clock face. ⑭ One of the strangest houses in the city, **No. 6 Nussbaumstrasse** keeps its delightful carved balconies in a tree-shaded corner. ⑮ Dramatic perspex sculptures and cashiers' desks make the **Hypotheken Bank** more like a house of modern art than of Mammon. ⑯ The colossal **Blumenstrasse fire station** makes an arresting sight.

▶ 86

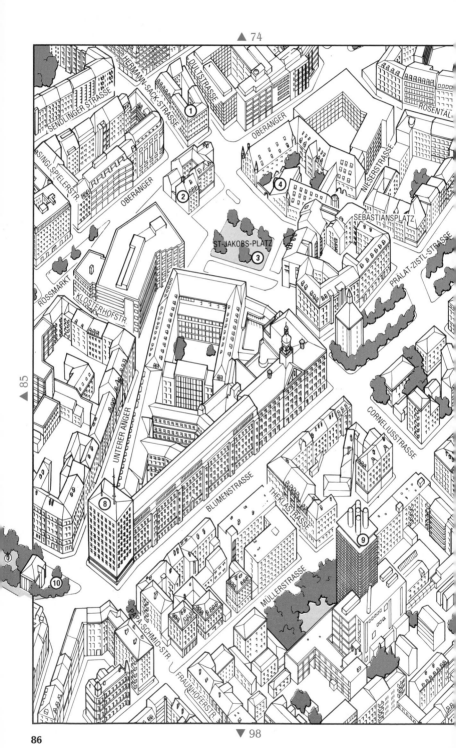

SENDLINGER STRASSE

HERMANN-SACK-STRASSE

DULTSTRASSE

OBERANGER

ROSENTAL

NIESERSTRASSE

ASING SPIELER STR.

OBERANGER

SEBASTIANSPLATZ

ST-JAKOBS-PLATZ

PRÄLAT-ZISTL-STRASSE

ROSSMARKT

KLOSTERHOFSTR.

UNTERER ANGER

CORNELIUSSTRASSE

BLUMENSTRASSE

THEKLASTRASSE

MÜLLERSTRASSE

PAPA-SCHMID-STR.

FRAUNHOFERSTR.

# Viktualienmarkt

A honeycomb of history, ① the **Altes Hackerhaus** (D) has four much-vaulted dining-rooms, with an atmosphere both barn-like and intimate. As far back as 1570, beer was brewed here by the Hacker family. Their name is still preserved in the giant Hacker-Pschorr brewery. ② The truncated green **Ignaz-Günther-Haus** was home to the sculptor of the same name until his death in 1775. His view today would be ③ the uninspiring **St-Jakobs-Platz** and the dramatically sloping roof of ④ the marvellous **Munich City Museum** (Münchner Stadtmuseum). Highlights here are a magical puppet collection, a massive brewing exhibition and beautifully reconstructed homes and taverns from centuries past (open Wednesdays till 8.30 pm). Also the marvellous wooden morris dancers of Erasmus Grasser (c. 1480). The clientele at the museum café (D) also merit study, perched on their minimalist furniture and grazing on olives, feta cheese and lean ham. ⑤ At the **Café Bar Eduscho** (D) you can buy fresh coffee (gorgeously packaged) to take home or to drink there, standing shoulder to shoulder with the buyers and traders at ⑥ the **Viktualienmarkt**. This is the city's most theatrical open-air market, a vast pile of fresh green, red and muddy brown. Some stalls sell 20 different types of potato, others 20 different herbs or 50 different kinds of sausage. ⑦ The statue of comedian **Karl Valentin** (water spouting from his cigarette) receives fresh flowers every morning from the market traders. Other entertainers thus commemorated are Ida Schumacher, Liesl Karlstadt, Elise Aulinger, Weiss Ferdl and Roider Jackl; it takes detective work to track them down. ⑧ The vast, orange brick fortress that is the **Town Planning Department** and ⑨ the nameless **green tower** with four smoke-billowing chimneys thrusting upwards from its roof. This is one of the municipal buildings that supplies hot water to radiators throughout the city. ⑩ The imposing Greek portico of the **Marionette Theatre** (1858, four matinées a week) belies the size of its small wooden performers. ⑪ **Gärtnerplatz** is a lovely, salmon-pink, circular delight, named after the court architect Friedrich von Gärtner (1792-1847), who designed the southern half of grandiose Ludwigstrasse after his predecessor Leo von Klenze had fallen out with King Ludwig I.

▶ 88

▲ 87

# The Isar Gate

① In a quiet corner just off the thronging Viktualienmarkt (*see page 87*) sits the **Weinschänke am Markt** (**D**), run by the Stoger family and serving with its *Bratwurst* a delicious cabbage filled with ham, black pepper and juniper berries. ② If you want to watch the market activity while eating, the **Gaststätte Stadt Kempten** (**D**) is a perfect vantage point. ③ In landlocked Munich, the **Poseidon** fish restaurant (**DD**) is a rarity. ④ The **Isartor** (1337), one of the original city gates, now housing a fascinating, quirky museum to the celebrated Munich comedian Karl Valentin. Open 11.01 am-5.29 pm, Mon, Tue, Fri and Sat; adults 2.99 DM, children 1.49 DM. Visit the café if you have time. ⑤ **Radlsteg** is a pretty little street dotted with antique shops and gold- and silversmiths, just off ⑥ **Tal**, meaning `valley', a broad, showpiece street. Shops include ⑦ **Piano Haus Lang**, selling beautiful keyboard instruments, ⑧ **Musik Rausch**, specialists in Bavarian instruments such as zithers, accordions and flutes, and ⑨ the plush **Studio 54**, a luxury bedding and drapes store. ⑩ **Teeschale** sells more than 100 different teas. ⑪ The **Halim** restaurant (**DD**) serves Thai and Indonesian food. ⑫ **Master's Home**, a bizarre basement bar with a ground floor entrance lobby that is deserted apart from a barber's chair and mirrors. ⑬ The **Rieger** fur shop, a hi-tech greenhouse on a painfully thin strip of parkland. ⑭ **Klenzestrasse**, named after the master architect Leo von Klenze, who designed some of Munich's greatest neoclassical buildings (Glyptothek, Alte Pinakothek, *see pages 49, 51*). ⑮ The speciality at the **Mai** (**DD**) Chinese restaurant is chicken with lemon grass and peppers: look out for the *trompe l'oeil* balcony. ⑯ **Harlekin** sells skimpy, glittering costumes for exotic dancers and strip-tease artistes. ⑰ **Bonacker-München** looks like a set for *The Merchant of Venice* and sells lush furnishing material. ⑱ Hundreds of oranges decorate the pretty **Vivaldi** (**DD**) pizzeria-restaurant. ⑲ **Herz-Jesu Klosterkirche** attached to a Catholic girls' hostel: no stained glass glories here, just three narrow windows set in the brickwork like stern little eyes. ⑳ **Joe Peñas**, a stylish café (**D**) serving up Mexican food and loud music. ㉑ **Hagen**, an earthy, popular music venue-cum-bistro (**D**). ㉒ Attractively renovated apartments at **No. 3 Kohlstrasse**. Don't miss the suspended aluminium-guttering windowboxes.

90 ▶

# St Lukas

▲ 79

► 92

▼ 103

① Sausage-lovers gather to buy the best at **Walter's Wurstladen**. ② One of the city's prettiest buildings, **Eduard-Hartmann-Haus**. Note the clock and belltower at its summit and the owl resting beneath one of the bay windows. ③ The massive **St Lukas** (1893-96) is another of Munich's giant churches, with an almost circular interior. ④ **Nos 2-6 Liebherrstrasse** make an impressive trio. Try crossing ⑤ little **Mariannenbrücke** on to ⑥ the elevated **weir walkway** down the middle of the Isar - it's unnerving but fun. ⑦ **Mühlen-Kaisergarten Studio**, a fragrant-smelling craft shop, specializing in wooden, hand-carved spice- and coffee-grinders. ⑧ The **Mutti Bräu im Lehel** (1907), a cheap but smart café-restaurant (**D**), with a lavish exterior depicting devils whispering into the ear of a wealthy man. ⑨ **No. 20 Thierschstrasse**, a characterful old block built in 1894 by J.M. Häusler, its grimy, red-brick exterior contrasting with the modern kitchen showroom on its ground floor. ⑩ Two magnificent muscular **satyrs** hold up the bay window of the house on the corner of Obermaierstrasse and Steinsdorfstrasse. The sculptor's name (A. Kaindl) is carved on one of the creatures' bows, and is just visible from the pavement. ⑪ The attractive **Galerie Erturk**, selling Oriental cushions and carpets. ⑫ **Ludwigsbrücke** is a busy road bridge, replacing one which was washed away in 1813 by the rampaging River Isar in the days before it was tamed by engineering and channelling. Some 100 onlookers were drowned in that disaster, prompting the eventual construction of a series of dams, canals and concrete bank-side reinforcements that today keep the Isar's ferocious potential in check. ⑬ The **Father Rhine Fountain** (Vater-Rhein-Brunnen, 1901) stands on an island in the middle of the Isar. The Rhine is personified by a wild, bearded figure pouring water out of a jug. ⑭ The stern-looking **Deutsches Museum Concert Hall**, recently renovated, has staged not just serious classical events but jazz and pop shows, too. ⑮ Perhaps Germany's most attractive indoor swimming pool, the **Müllersches-Volksbad**. Built between 1897 and 1907, this large, elegant complex is dominated by a graceful white and gold clock tower. The style is *Jugendstil*, Germany's art nouveau, and the Volksbad is considered the most beautiful of its kind.

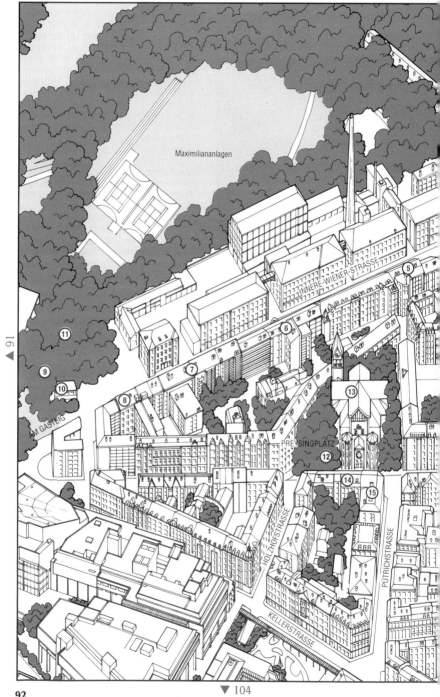

Maximilananlagen

INNERE-WIENER-STRASSE

AM GASTEIG

PREYSINGPLATZ

HOLZHOFSTRASSE

PUTRICHSTRASSE

KELLERSTRASSE

# Wiener Platz

▲ 81

① The pretty little **Weinhäusl** restaurant (**DD**), an Alpine cottage in the middle of town, sets the rural tone for the Wiener Platz. ② Green and brown **market traders' huts** add colour and charm. ③ The **Hofbräukeller** (**D**) is a giant, smoky cavern; ④ the **Café Wiener Platz** (**D**) an up-market student haunt, where everyone smokes and talks and flicks their hair back with great intensity. The north side of the Innere Wiener Strasse is nothing but crumbling factories and building sites, but the south side has a surprising smattering of cheap, interesting restaurants, among them ⑤ **Bernard and Bernard** (**D**), open from 7 pm each night, serving a huge range of crêpes (with names such as Carnac, Jamaica, Guadeloupe); most seem to involve Grand Marnier or cognac. Further along the road ⑥ at No. 18, the **Niawaran** (**DD**) serves Iranian dishes, in which the most common ingredients are spinach, aubergine, yoghurt and lamb. ⑦ **Zoo** pet shop, with baby rabbits in the window and tropical fish in tanks which take up one entire wall of the shop. ⑧ A cherub in the window is the only indication of the downstairs **Preysing Keller** (**DDD**), the smartest cellar restaurant in Munich, serving *haute cuisine* beneath a high-vaulted ceiling. Here the seafood lives in an aquarium and the customers live on rarefied specialities such as goose liver pâté, venison steak *tartare* and pigeons in basil sauce. ⑨ The original **St Nicholas Church** used to be the focal point for the city's medieval leper colony; it was rebuilt in the 16thC. ⑩ **Altöttinger Chapel** (1678) next door is worth visiting for its astonishing collection of giant ornate candles, kept behind glass. ⑪ Large numbers of cyclists use this point of entry to the rolling, riverside parkland of the **Maximiliananlagen** (*see page 81*). ⑫ A small **statue** of two weary bricklayers stands on the small patch of pedestrianized Preysingstrasse outside ⑬ **St Johannes Church**. ⑭ **Café Stöpsel** (**D**) provides loud rock music and breakfast for bleary students. ⑮ The trendy **Kuczinsky** bar-restaurant (**DD**) has the day's specials written with studied casualness across the mirrors. Beware: cocktails cost as much as the food.

▼ 105

# Goetheplatz

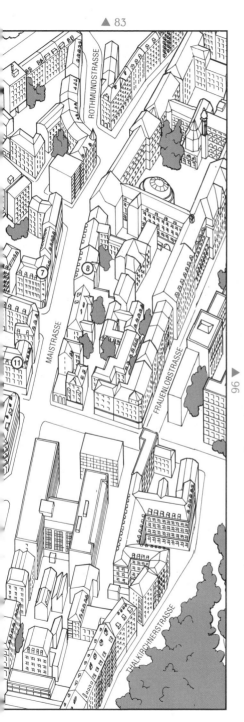

① The long, broad boulevard of **Lindwurm-strasse** is a joy for cyclists. ② Outside the **Children's Hospital** (Kinderspital) at No. 4 Lindwurmstrasse stand two charming statues, one of Little Red Riding Hood with food-filled picnic basket, about to pat the wolf, the other of a small boy accompanied by a rabbit and Puss-in-Boots. ③ Over the road, the **Café-Konditorei Lander** sells marvellous chocolate pear cake and sticky Florentines. ④ The six-screen **Royal Filmpalast** is one of Munich's biggest and ugliest cinemas, matching Goetheplatz itself, which like many Munich squares has been rebuilt from the ruins of World War II with a view more to function than form. ⑤ An exception is the curving exterior of the **Goetheplatz Post Office**, a stylish echo of the 1930s, while ⑥ the **escalators** up from the U-bahn station are a glimpse of the future: immobile when not needed, they go either up or down on demand. Feeding into Goetheplatz are a number of streets bearing the names of composers. Among these is Mozartstrasse, at the end of which, within walking distance, stands the Theresienwiese, the massive showground which each year stages the world's greatest beer pageant, the Oktoberfest. ⑦ The **Nam Long** (DD) is one of the city's few Vietnamese restaurants, and ⑧ the **Lebensmittel** in Maistrasse one of the city's few Greek supermarkets. ⑨ Automatic doors give access to the **Klösterl-Apotheke**, a modern, designer setting for ancient homeopathic remedies. ⑩ A three-storey mural on the wall of a sewing-machine shop shows a rather hungry-looking cat peering up at birds in a tree. ⑪ **Zöttl** is a thriving supermarket and baker's, displaying in its window alone some 22 different breads. ⑫ At the **Sato Restaurant** (D), diners enjoy delicious Turkish grills, while across the road, in the basement of a pink apartment block, ⑬ the **Galaxie** Greek restaurant (D) serves food from the other side of the Aegean. Doubtless ingredients for both restaurants come from ⑭ the **Akbulut grocery**, an aromatic emporium piled high with olives, tomatoes and huge boxes of Turkish delight. Just at the bottom of Häberlstrasse is the beautifully-preserved Paulaner brewery. ⑮ From her cramped little shop, **Rosemarie Kirchner** sells ecclesiastical candles that range from small, unadorned specimens to glorious creations the size of a gatepost, vivid with red, bleeding hearts or representations of the Virgin Mary.

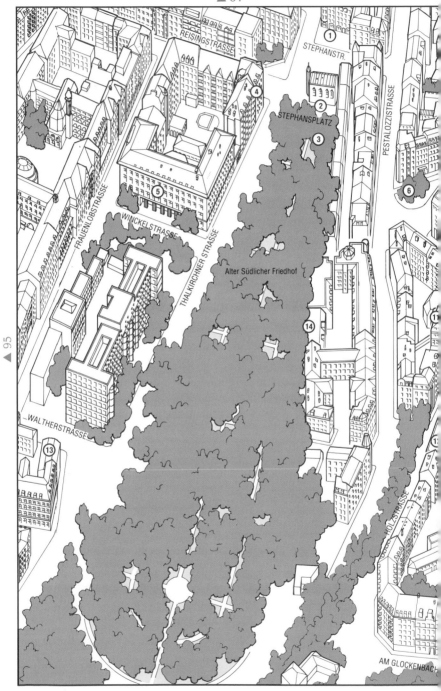

REISINGSTRASSE

STEPHANSTR.

① ②

PESTALOZZISTRASSE

STEPHANSPLATZ

④

③

⑥

⑤

FRAUENLOBSTRASSE

WINCKELSTRASSE

THALKIRCHNER STRASSE

Alter Südlicher Friedhof

⑭

⑪

WALTHERSTRASSE

⑬

⑫

HOLZSTRASSE

AM GLOCKENBACH

# The Old Southern Cemetery

① On a patch of pavement outside a florist's stands Konstantin Frick's alarming green, brain-like **sculpture** (1980). More apocalyptic visions are displayed across the road, on the bronze doors of ② **St Stephan's Church** (1576): giants casting down boulders from the heavens, while on earth a skeleton rides a horse through mass slaughter and chaos. This pretty, onion-domed church is the chapel to the next-door ③ **Alter Südlicher Friedhof** (Old Southern Cemetery), built in the 16thC to house the city's plague victims (when this land was outside city boundaries). The cemetery's ageing tombstones cast an eerie reflection in the plate glass windows of ④ the **Demos** construction company's headquarters. ⑤ Grim-browed, stone-hewn heads of distinguished scientists thrust out from above the pillars that support the university **Pathology Institute**. ⑥ At the meeting of three small streets stands a dovecote-like **gents' lavatory**, discreetly shielded by trees. ⑦ For many years **Hans-Sachs-Strasse** has been a focal point for Munich's gay community. The west side of the street has an interesting array of establishments: ⑧ the so-understated-it's-almost-invisible **Matoi** Japanese restaurant (**DDD**), ⑨ the colourful **Modernes Theater** fringe theatre and coffee bar, and ⑩ the **Air Mail** boutique, selling a range of aggressively unisex clothes. Dominating the cobbled junction of Holzstrasse and Wester-mühlstrasse is ⑪ the attractively ribbed **Zettler** electrical factory. ⑫ The little **Süd Tirol** wine shop, decked out in Alpine flowers and quotations from the Greek writer Plutarch, such as "Wine The Wonderful Medicine". ⑬ On the west side of the cemetery, the bright yellow, blue and white **Weisses Bräuhaus-Stüberl** lends a touch of gaiety to this rather gloomy area: its merry little beer garden is the perfect antidote to the sombre avenues of the cemetery, where on the eastern side, ⑭ **towering gravestones** block out the view from the back windows of houses in Pestalozzistrasse. There is some compensation for the residents, though: from the front of their houses they have a clear view of the attractive little Westermühlbach, once part of a thriving canal network used by timber barges. Nowadays, in the old canal workers' houses down Jahnstrasse, intriguing new businesses thrive: ⑮ **Larifari's** at **No. 37** sells pre-war toys, including tin racing cars and a doll's house kitchen of the 1930s, complete with miniature tins of Nescafé.

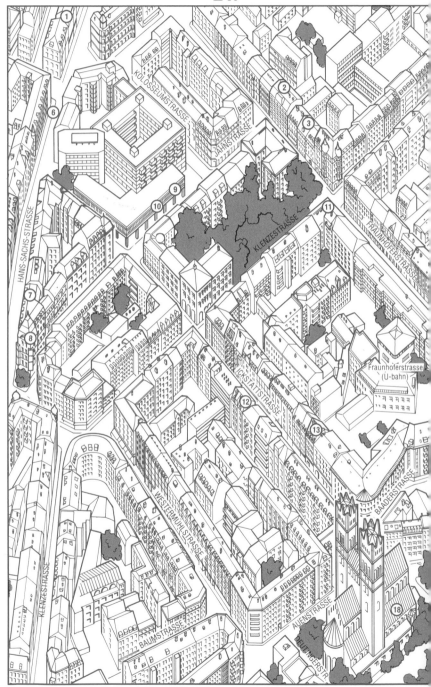

# Fraunhoferstrasse

① The **Puppenklinik** offers Munich's antique dolls a repair service: some of the more successful patients are displayed in the window. The shows at ② the **Werkstattkino** (Workshop Cinema) are definitely not for children - underground films with lashings of sex and the surreal. Homely apple strudel is on offer at ③ the cosy **Kaffeekuchl**, while light opera is the usual fare at ④ the handsome white **Gärtnerplatz Theatre**, built in 1864. After shows, the stars slip across the road to ⑤ the **Restaurant Theaterstube (DD)**, to devour shrimps on toast and butter behind its frosted glass windows. ⑥ Entering **Hans-Sachs-Strasse** (*see pages 97-8*), you are in alternative Munich. Towards ⑦ the south-eastern end of the street is an ever-changing collection of **shops** selling bric-à-brac, new and second-hand clothes, solar energy systems and halogen lights. ⑧ Landmark for the area is the pale cream **Together** disco, which sits on the corner of the street beneath a rather respectable-looking block of flats. ⑨ Supplying the area's record needs is the stark, thumping **Optimal**, set in a shabby, poster-covered shopping arcade next to ⑩ the **Feinkost grocery**, which sells Italian and South American specialities (fresh *pesto* thus rubs shoulders with Argentinian wine and Mexican *tequila*). ⑪ Strictly Bavarian pleasures are offered at **Engelbert Wandinger**, a *café-konditorei* where you can scoff creamy cakes while marvelling at the place's museum-like collection of coffee grinders. ⑫ Stroll into the back of **No. 18 Ickstattstrasse** and you will find one of the most attractive, creeper-strewn car service centres you are ever likely to see. ⑬ Over the road at No. 13, the **Schwimmkrabbe** restaurant offers basic décor but a rich selection of Turkish wines (D). ⑭ At one of the tables in the ultra-modern **Café Rischart** stands an eerie, white statue of a man drinking coffee. Another other-worldly experience is to take ⑮ the little **capsule lift** down into the bowels of Fraunhoferstrasse U-bahn station. ⑯ Back up on ground level, you might visit the small, pavilion-like **public lavatory** at the beginning of Reichenbach Bridge, then take a stroll ⑰ along the **wooded path** beside the River Isar. The same trees that cast a pleasant shade over the promenaders seem to be devouring ⑱ **St Maximilian Church**, built in 1901 and now benefitting from recent restoration.

▶ 100

BAADERSTRASSE

CORNELIUSSTRASSE

ERHARDTSTRASSE

CORNELIUSBRÜCKE

ISAR

REICHENBACHBRÜCKE

EDUARD-SCHMID-STRASSE

BEREITERANGER

MARIAHILFSTRASSE

# Ehrhardtstrasse and the River Isar

▲ 89

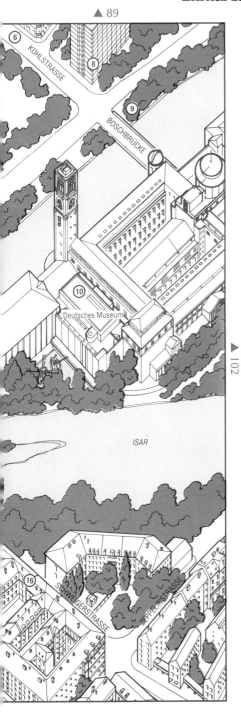

Behind the pretty net curtains of ① the **Isbuschka** restaurant (DD), vodka, bortsch, caviar and other Russian dishes are served. Across the road, tastes of a different kind are catered for at ② **Cornelius Men**, a group of three very smart and highly discreet shops selling clothes, books and videos for gay men. ③ **Bidjanbek** have an arresting collection of surreal pottery and sculptures. ④ **A. Lieben** specialize in English leather furniture: their sofas are virtual replicas of the benches on which Members of Parliament sit in London's House of Commons. Huge silver balls dwarf passers-by at the entrance to ⑤ the vast **European Patents Office**. Built between 1975 and 1980 and situated on a car-roaring stretch of the river embankment, this gigantic building is best viewed from the side in ⑥ **Kohlstrasse**, where it is masked by creepers and by ⑦ a dramatic metal **sculpture** which looks like two mechanical hammers fighting it out. Over the road stands ⑧ the **German Patent Office**, an unimaginative orange rectangle built between 1953 and 1959. ⑨ The stern-faced **statue of Otto von Bismarck** (1815-1898) presents a forbidding aspect to visitors crossing the small bridge to ⑩ the **German Museum of Science and Technology** (Deutsches Museum, *see page 103*). The museum (open daily) is huge fun to visit. ⑪ From the **Cornelius Bridge** (1901), you get a fine view into the Deutsches Museum's back yard (glimpses of fighter planes and windmills), and from ⑫ the pavement in front of **Nos 7-9 Ehrhardtstrasse** you can best appreciate the prosperous, bulging frontages of these prestigiously-positioned apartments. ⑬ The **Reichenbach Bridge** is a busy, six-lane beast, transporting one from the big-city atmosphere of the north bank to the more easy-going environment that is the southern half of the city. Looking south from the bridge, the skyline is dominated by the spire of the Mariahilfplatz Church, scene of the twice-a-year flea market and fair, the Auer Dult. ⑭ A leafy **riverside walk** takes one past ⑮ a **giant chess board**, on which players move pieces the size of traffic cones, close to which, to Cornelius Bridge, close to which is ⑯ the extraordinary **Galerie Z**, promoters of modern art that is challenging, to say the least. One of their exhibitors' works that attracted great attention from passers-by was a hammer embedded in their shattered window.

▶ 102

# Deutsches Museum

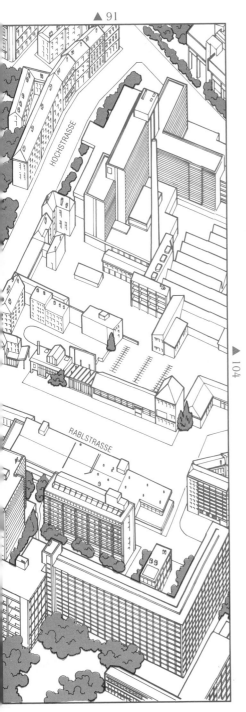

▶ 104

① Sitting upon an entire island in the middle of the River Isar, the vast **Deutsches Museum** (open daily 9 am-5 pm) is the answer to every child's rainy day. Despite being saddled with the title of `German Museum for Masterworks of Science and Technology', the place takes a show business approach to the problems of the universe, seeking to involve visitors by means of hands-on experiments and exhibits, rather than the hands-off, stay-behind-the-red-rope approach so familiar to museumgoers. Among the 15,000 items on show are the first German submarine, a fleet of gleaming vintage cars, the monoplane which Bleriot flew across the Channel and the very table upon which the atom was first split. Founded in 1903 by Oskar von Miller, the museum was badly damaged during World War II. A Latin inscription at the top of ② the **ornate entrance tower** explains that the museum was `restored from the ruins' in 1951. The museum is joined by a short bridge to the southern river bank and the area known as Au. ③ The **Schorschi Dog Salon** provides a striking reminder of Münchners' fondness for their four-legged friends, who are allowed to sit in many a respectable restaurant and for whom one must pay a child's fare on public transport. ④ **Lilienstrasse** possesses an appealing, sinuous shape, adorned by cherry trees and dominated by a distant view of the yellow-brick Volksbad baths. In summer the street also plays host to tables from ⑤ **Peppermint Park**, which spreads its customers out into the streets. Few people take notice of the simple **Auia-Brunnen** fountain ⑥ (Ludwig Schwanthaler, 1848), which features a young woman whose modesty befits the area's unpretentious atmosphere. ⑦ The tiny houses at **Nos 11 and 11a Franz-Prûller-Strasse** speak volumes about Au's modest expectations compared to those of its smarter sibling across the river. However, an upbringing here looks as if it might be rather fun. Next to ⑧ the pretty little **Kegelhof playground** stands ⑨ the **Jugendtreff kindergarten**, perched excitingly above a rushing stream. At this point Quellerstrassse downgrades from a road to ⑩ a **riverside walkway**, while Wilhelm-Herbert-Weg leads promisingly up to ⑪ **Hochstrasse**, where unfortunately trees deny a view over Au to all but employees of ⑫ the high-rise **BSHG** factory.

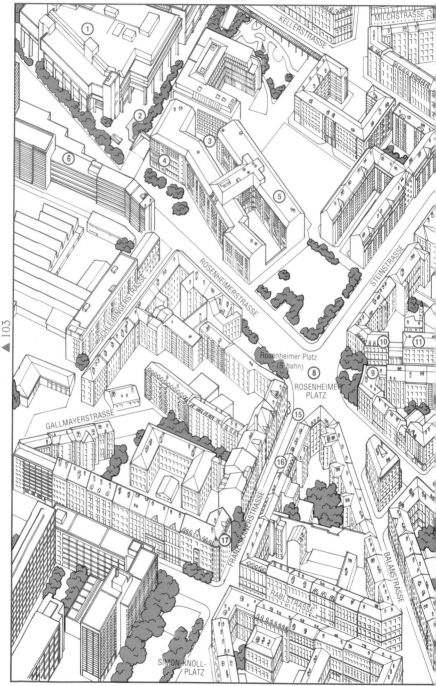

MILCHSTRASSE

KELLERSTRASSE

ROSENHEIMERSTRASSE

SCHLEIBINGERSTRASSE

STEINSTRASSE

Rosenheimer Platz
(S-bahn)

ROSENHEIMER
PLATZ

GALLMAYERSTRASSE

FRANZISKANERSTRASSE

BALANSTRASSE

RABLSTRASSE

SIMON-KNOLL-
PLATZ

# Rosenheimer Platz

① One of the least popular additions to the Munich skyline is the **Gasteig Cultural Centre** (1985), which houses concert halls, a studio theatre, the city library and the Philharmonic Orchestra within its walls. However, the severity of the architecture here is somewhat reduced by the presence of some rather playful sculptures that give the concrete monster some personality. ② One of these is an **upturned tuba**, created by Albert Hien in 1989, and also serving as a fountain; the other is ③ a **gear lever** that has folded up on itself. This is the view that meets guests staying at ④ the **City Hilton Hotel** as they draw back their curtains of a morning. This and ⑤ the adjoining **Bayerische Hausbau** development, an estate of private apartment blocks, have been built in the same blue and grey tones. ⑥ The glass-coated **Motorama** building represents the German 20thC version of an Eastern bazaar: long rows of car dealers all under one roof, Porsches vying with Ladas for purchasers. ⑦ At this junction, the **Amaranth** restaurant (**DD**) offers hungry wayfarers not Munich's usual feast of flesh, but a vegetarian-only menu, featuring such delicacies as asparagus risotto; pottery window-boxes bearing the restaurant's name are a pretty touch. ⑧ **Rosenheimer Platz** is another car-dominated junction, in itself unattractive, but the parent of some interesting side streets. Pedestrianized Weissenburger Strasse carries the most appeal, with ⑨ its **Pizzeria Bella Italia** (**D**), ⑩ the smarter **Dal Cavaliere** (a pizzeria-restaurant, no less,**DD**) opposite the **Café-Eis Philharmonie** (**D**) ice-cream parlour. ⑪ Further down the street, **Erwin Kronawitter's** old-fashioned establishment sells brushes for everything from painting masterpieces to sweeping floors. ⑫ **Weissenburger Platz** itself is one of Munich's few genuinely pretty squares, boasting lavish flowerbeds, a circular shape and green chairs that look like rubbish bins but have a pleasant give to them. From these, you can glimpse ⑬ the attractive, tree-lined **Lothringer Strasse** and ⑭ **Antiquariat**, selling beautiful old books and prints. Franziskanerstrasse has traffic but some unexpected treasures: ⑮ above No. 3 Franziskanerstrasse is the **statue of a rent collector**, money-bag full but with hand stretched out for more. ⑯ **No. 11** has elegant gold discs dotted across its wrought-iron balconies and ⑰ **Kunst und Präsent** sell pretty little gifts.

# Haidhausen

① The spartan **Diyar Restaurant** (D), serving Kurdish specialities, makes a suitably bizarre introduction to Haidhausen, the area touted by many as Munich's new artists' quarter. Construction of Haidhausen's gracious apartment blocks began following the defeat of the French army in 1871. Many of the streets bear French names as a reminder of victories during that campaign. The grandest square is ② **Bordeauxplatz**, a flower-dotted, hippodrome-shaped area, encircled by tram lines and with a little Italian wine shop ③ **Grenzgänger** at one end and ④ **Der Drachenladen**, selling luminous dayglo kites, at the other. ⑤ **Orleansplatz** is less blessed. The ugly ⑥ **Kaufring** department store dominates the square's northern end, while ⑦ a large **maroon lift** down to the U-Bahn is the only discernible feature on this windswept patch of ground. More friendly to both eye and passer-by are ⑧ the **Ostbahnhof** (East Station), a compact, rectangular package of a building, stuffed with fragrant fast-food counters, and ⑨ the tempting **Ostbahnhof-Bäckerei**, a café-cum-baker's shop just off the square. ⑩ A hundred yards down the street, **Pariser Platz** is built on a more human scale, and neighbourhood walkers and talkers gather to scoff either sumptuous Coppa Grand Marnier at ⑪ the **Eiscafé Venezia** or chicken curry at ⑫ the **Kashmir Restaurant** in nearby Pariser Strasse (**DD**). The shops on Weissenburger Strasse are a pretty mainstream collection, with the exception of ⑬ **Binner's Beinkleider**, offering some rather smart men's and women's clothes at prices struggling artists might not be able to afford. More humbly-priced pleasures are available in Pariser Strasse: ⑭ **Teeladen** stock 220 different teas and 40 varieties of honey; ⑮ the **Café-Bar Halifax** (**DD**) is a large, dark-wooden establishment serving specialities not from Yorkshire but from Italy. ⑯ On the corner of Lothringer Strasse, a **bright yellow house** (perfectly matching its next-door tree) accommodates a Greek delicatessen which displays ouzo in bottles surrounded by plastic, Parthenon-type pillars. ⑰ At **Würzburger Hof** (D) football fans meet to discuss the fortunes of the city's top soccer team Bayern Munich in the national *Bundesliga*, while next door, separated by a riot of ivy, ⑱ Irwin and Uschi Luckas offer darts and *Weisswurst* in a snug little spot called **Achterdeck** (D), lit by pottery lamps.

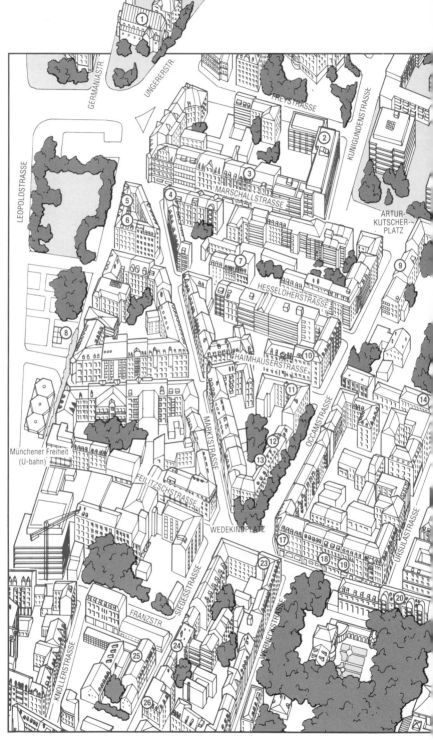

GERMANIASTR.

UNGERERSTR.

FREYSTRASSE

KUNIGUNDENSTRASSE

LEOPOLDSTRASSE

MARSCHALLSTRASSE

ARTUR-
KUTSCHER-
PLATZ

HESSELOHERSTRASSE

HAIMHAUSERSTRASSE

OCCAMSTRASSE

URSULASTRASSE

MARKTSTRASSE

Münchener Freiheit
(U-bahn)

FEILITZSCHSTRASSE

WEDEKINDPLATZ

SIEGESSTRASSE

FRANZSTR.

WERNECKSTRASSE

KNOLLERSTRASSE

# Schwabing

Schwabing is Greenwich Village without the grime, the Left Bank without the tourists. Historically it has been home to artists, writers and intellectuals, including Bertolt Brecht, Thomas Mann and Henrik Ibsen. Lenin lived here for two years and set up his revolutionary journal *Iskra*. Today, smart boutiques have squeezed out many of the more struggling artists, but the area still retains a youthful, bohemian atmosphere, especially after sundown. ① **St Erlös Church** has a strange, almost childish clock and an interior decorated with similar patterns. ② The new grey-and-green **Hotel Residence** has been skilfully grafted on to Schwabing. ③ The **Fertl** cycle shop is announced by a model of a fat man on a bike, poking out of a first-floor wall. ④ **Pavone** sells decorative art lamps and the like. Over the road are two of the area's multitudinous music clubs, ⑤ **The Roxx** and ⑥ **P.M.** ⑦ **Theater Scaramouche**, one of Munich's smarter fringe theatres. ⑧ **Münchener Freiheit Forum**, a rather shabby pedestrian precinct containing shops, cafés, drunks and giant chess boards. ⑨ **Bass Underground** looks like an air raid shelter but is in fact a jazz and country-and-western venue. ⑩ **Voyage** offers a short, tasty French menu in civilized surroundings (**DD**). ⑪ At **Novaks**, the proud boast is that they have staged live music (middle-of-the-road) for 25 years. ⑫ The sign at the entrance to the **Turbo** disco reads: `Stop - We Play Oldies'. Next door is ⑬ **Albatros**, another disco that is just as loud. ⑭ The home of the **Münchner Lach- und Schiessgesellschaft** (Laugh And Shoot) political cabaret company, familiar faces on German TV. ⑮ **Mutti Bräu**, a pleasant eating and drinking spot with a long-standing reputation (**DD**). ⑯ Perched on a raised square, **St Sylvester Church** dominates the whole area in an avuncular way. ⑰ **Jetset** sells clothes that range from the bright to the flashy. ⑱ **Simone Tanner**, ⑲ **Oscar** and ⑳ **Vibration**, three smart and expensive shops in extremely up-market Feilitzchstrasse. ㉑ **El Cortijo**, a Spanish restaurant specializing in fish (**DD**). ㉒ **Coté Sud**, a smart French restaurant serving an inventive range of food (**DD**). ㉓ **Roucka**, at 50 metres (150 feet) surely the longest modern art emporium in Munich. ㉔ **Blue Nile**, one of the city's handful of African restaurants (**DD**). ㉕ **tomate**, a well-known disco-cum-pub. ㉖ **Podium**, one of Schwabing's longest-established venues for pop, rhythm and blues, jazz and rock.

# Outside Munich

### Outside Munich: Ludwig II's palaces

The spirit of 'mad' King Ludwig II of Bavaria (1864-1886) lives on in the three fairy-tale 'palaces' he built to the south of Munich. For most visitors, a visit to Munich is not a real visit to Munich unless it also includes an expedition to one, at least, of these out-of-town attractions, all easy day trips.

In terms of splendour and magnificence, Ludwig modelled himself on France's great 'Sun King', Louis XIV. He was passionate about art and music and took the great composer Richard Wagner both under his wing and into his household. Together, he envisaged, they would make Munich the musical capital of the world. However, his wild schemes bankrupted the Bavarian treasury, and in 1886 he was declared insane and sent to a castle on the edge of Starnberger Lake (Starnbergersee). A few days later his fully-clothed body was found floating in the lake. How he met his death is still a mystery.

### Neuschwanstein

A white-turreted fantasy, built in early medieval style and dramatically positioned overlooking a gorge and lake. The model upon which Walt Disney based the Disneyland fairy-tale castle. Highlights are the throne room and the Singers' Hall (Sängersaal). Half a mile away is the castle of Hohenschwangau (many Wagner memorabilia), from where Ludwig and his protegé watched Neuschwanstein being built. Take a train from Hauptbahnhof to Füssen (2 hours), then a bus to Hohenschwangau (5 minutes). By car, take the B12 to Landsberg am Lech, then the B17 to Füssen.

### Linderhof

Ludwig's version of the Petit Trianon at Versailles, and the only one of his creations to be completed during his lifetime. Stroll around the beautifully laid-out gardens and don't miss the lavish Moorish pavilion and the extraordinary Venus Grotto, with its artificial lake and waterfall. Ludwig used to drift across the water in a swan-shaped craft. While in the area, it is well worth going to the beautiful little valley town of Ettal (7 miles away), with its stout-walled 14thC monastery (Kloster Ettal); also Oberammergau, where every ten years the Passion Play (Passionsspiele) is performed. The first performance of the play was given in 1633, in thanks to God for ending the plague. To get to Ettal, take the B2, then turn off on the B23; Schloss Linderhof is 7 miles to the west, Oberammergau to the north.

### Herrenchiemsee
A small island named Herreninsel, in the western half of Bavaria's biggest lake, Chiemsee, is the site for this, the last of Ludwig's projects (work began in 1878). Herrenchiemsee was his most extravagant and sumptuous palace, an attempt to re-create the glory of his namesake Louis XIV's Versailles. The real jewel of the palace is the breathtaking Hall of Mirrors (Spiegelsaal), which measures more than 100 yards in length and which is the setting for candle-lit concerts during the summer months. A ferry operates from the small harbour at Stock, taking visitors also to the smaller island of Fraueninsel, where there are some delightful little fishermen's cottages as well as an attractive Benedictine convent, founded in the 8thC; note the 13thC frescos. To get there by car, take the A8 towards Salzburg and turn off after about 50 miles at Prien.

The castles are open daily, from 8.30 am-5.30 pm (Apr-Sep) and 10 am-4 pm (Oct-Mar). In summer, day trips to all the castles are operated by Panorama Tours, 8 Arnulfstrasse; tel. 598160. Prices start at 75 DM (children 35 DM) including admission to sights.

### Dachau
Twelve miles north-west of Munich stands Dachau, an attractive little hillside town of 35,000 people, which used to be a favourite haunt of Bavarian artists, and has a history even older than Munich's, stretching back to the 9thC AD. Today, however, it is better known to the world as the location of the infamous Nazi concentration camp where 32,000 people died between 1933 and 1945. Housed in a disused gunpowder factory, Dachau was the prototype for all Hitler's later camps, although it was

not an extermination camp itself. There is now a museum on the site (KZ-Gedenkstätte, open 9 am-5 pm, Tue-Sun, entrance free) to commemorate the camp's victims. Exhibits include photographs, uniforms, contemporary documents, and the insignia that identified the prisoners: black for political prisoners, pink for homosexuals and yellow for Jews.

To get to the museum, take the S-2 train to Dachau (a 20-minute ride) and then the 722 bus to the Gedenkstätte. By car, take the B304. The town itself is also worth visiting, for its pretty 18thC façades and for the one remaining wing of its rather grand castle (Schloss Dachau), built in 1715 by Josef Effner to replace the original 16thC structure. Just east of Dachau is the elgant Schloss Schleissheim complex (S-1 train, get off at Oberschleissheim); here three airy palaces sit in large, well-disciplined gardens.

# T HE
# I NDEXES

# INDEX OF GENERAL POINTS OF INTEREST

# N

# T

# INDEX OF PEOPLE OF INTEREST

# INDEX OF STREET NAMES

# Z

# Munich U-Bahn and S-Bahn system map

**Page numbers of isometric maps on which the stations are featured**

**U-Bahn**

**S-Bahn**

| | |
|---|---|
| **geplant** | (projected) |
| **im Bau** | (under construction) |
| **P → R** | Park & Ride |
| **Mo-Fr zeitweise** | Restricted service Mon-Fri; no service at weekends. |
| **ab 1993** | from 1993 |

MVV

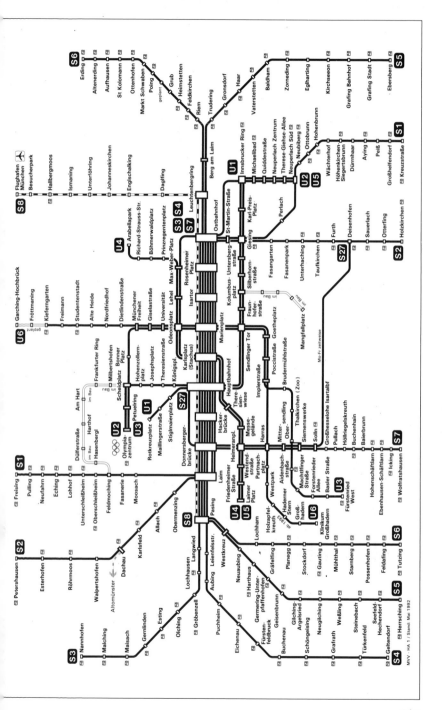

MVV · HA 1 / Stand: Mai 1992